SOAR

IN HIS STRENGTH

Volume 1

Danny Thornton

Dedication and Acknowledgments

I am so thankful to the Holy Spirit for allowing me to pen down His thoughts with mine to create this sixty-day devotional. It would be proper to dedicate this first volume to Him and His special presence that rests upon me as I awkwardly hit the letters on my keyboard. It is a unique experience that prompts me to write more often. I would also like to thank Him for the discipline necessary to accomplish this. I am humbled that You would partner with me in my life and exploits.

I would also like to thank my lovely bride, Jean Marie, who I married forty-nine years ago. Thank you for freeing me up not just to write this but for releasing me to preach the gospel around the world.

I also want to dedicate this to my grandchildren, whom I love dearly. I hope that through these devotionals, you will sense what the Holy Spirit has done in me and the legacy that is yours.

Finally, I would like to thank my two gospel sons, Pastor Dan Allen and Pastor Justin Metcalf, for trusting and honoring me as a voice in their life. I love you, and I am so very proud of you both.

Contents

But they that wait upon the LORD
shall renew their strength;
they shall mount up with wings as eagles;
they shall run, and not be weary;
and they shall walk, and not faint.

Isaiah 40:31

Introduction

But they that wait upon the Lord shall renew their
strength; they shall mount up with wings as eagles; they
shall run, and not be weary; and they shall walk, and not
faint. (Isaiah 40:31 KJV)

The ultimate transfer of God's strength began in your life when you
asked Jesus Christ to be your Lord and Savior. Instantly, His Holy
Spirit came into your spirit and formed the greatest fusion of power the
world can never offer. It is through this union with God that we receive
the strength necessary to face each day.

The word *strength* can be defined as the quality or state of being
strong. Just as our physical body needs nourishment for strength, we
must also feed our spirit the necessary nutrients to properly strengthen
our day. Look at this passage:

The human spirit can endure a sick body, but who can
bear a crushed spirit? (Proverbs 18:14 NLT).

My hope is that these devotionals will strengthen your spirit so you
can SOAR throughout your day and be able to stay above your problems—not for your problems to stay above you!

What is it that you expect to receive when you read a devotional? Do
you want to be inspired to move forward in what God called you to do?
Is it to fulfill a deep desire to be more like Jesus in your behavior or is it
to be strengthened and encouraged for your day ahead?

It may be all of the above, and if it is, then you have the right devotional in your hands. *Soar in His Strength* was written and designed to usher God's strength into your spirit so you can be encouraged in your walk with God.

My hope and desire is that this book will inspire you to be the best mom, dad, sister, brother, business person, preacher, pastor, man, woman, or young person you can be. Many of these devotions contain my own stories and experiences that directly relate to the scripture for the day.

I pray that my personal journey will help you avoid unnecessary hardships as you receive understanding through each devotional. To have *understanding* means to have the power to comprehend.

In 1 Chronicles 12:32 (KJV), the sons of Issachar were said to have an "understanding of the times." They joined David in a town called Ziglag with others who had fled the rule of King Saul. I'm sure David was blessed to have them for their insight. I hope that these devotionals will do the same for you: that you will receive an understanding of the times you live in to help you make proper decisions.

I added pinpoint questions to cause you to think. That's right, "think." I want you to think about your relationship with the Holy Spirit and other relationships in your life; think about your behavior; think for the good of others, and not just yourself. Above all, I pray you will yield to the mind of Christ and not your carnal mind.

To get the best use of *Soar in His Strength* devotional, I recommend that you:

- Ask the Holy Spirit for the right time to do your devotions. (I recommend at the very start of your day)
- Do your best to make your appointment with God and keep it, but do not be legalistic.

- Shut the door as Jesus said in Matthew 6:6 concerning entering your prayer closet. To me, that means to turn off every device that will distract you, including your TV and phone.
- Before you begin your devotional, ask the Holy Spirit to open your spirit to receive the understanding you need.
- Always be bold and ask the Holy Spirit tough questions and expect Him to answer in your spirit.
- Lastly, bring a pen and paper with you to jot down anything you are impressed to write. It might be the Holy Spirit prompting you!

My hope and prayer is that you will develop a Holy-Spirit-empowered life. Somebody Believe!

Day 1: How Do You See Yourself?

And there came an angel of the Lord, and sat under an oak which was in Ophrah, that pertained unto Joash the Abiezrite: and his son Gideon threshed wheat by the winepress, to hide it from the Midianites. And the angel of the Lord appeared unto him, and said unto him, The Lord is with thee, thou mighty man of valour. (Judges 6:11-12 KJV)

If you take the time to read the rest of the story, you will notice that Gideon was reluctant to respond to the angel. If I were the one to write it, I would say it in my vernacular "Whoa, angel dude, you talking to me? Seriously, me? This is crazy, man!" You see, Gideon had a very difficult time seeing himself as a mighty man of valor. But here's the thing; Gideon couldn't see himself as a mighty man of valor. At least not until God revealed it to him. And it's the same for you. You need a revelation from the Holy Spirit to convince you that you are a child of God.

Listen, Champion, you are now facing a brand new day. You may face some brand-new problems or challenges today. So why not get a new perspective of yourself through God's eyes? I am certain that God sees you much differently than you see yourself. Do you remember the Israelites when they were spying out the Promised Land? They had an unhealthy mental vision of themselves, I call it, "the insect mentality." Who cares about insects, right? Not too many people. If you think that way about yourself, others will too.

> And there we saw the giants, the sons of Anak, which come
> of the giants: and we were in our own sight as grasshoppers,
> and so we were in their sight. (Numbers 13:33 KJV)

The way you see yourselves is the way others will. So if you want to see yourself the way God sees you, then you have to do something about it.

Let me share my secret for how I train my mind to get a new perspective of myself. When I get caught up in negative thinking, and a feeling of insignificance or dread begins to come over me like a blanket, I do something about it the minute I become aware of it. If I don't, I will become one of Satans POWs (Prisoner of War). In our arm forces, soldiers are trained that if they are ever captured, they are only to give their name, rank, and serial number. They do this for a few reasons. One reason would be that our troops would not give out any secret information regarding our strategy. Another reason is that the soldier will remind himself who he is and who he belongs to. The enemy's goal is to strip you of your identity. Satan tried this to Jesus in the wilderness.

> During that time the devil came and said to him, "If
> you are the Son of God, tell these stones to become
> loaves of bread." (Matthew 4:3 NLT)

He wanted Jesus to question His identity and to whom He belonged. It's the same with you. If Satan can get you to question your identity, you will forget to whom you belong and that you are a child of God.

So when the enemy comes to bind me by using my feelings or sending a spirit of condemnation on me for my imperfections, I turn and confess: "My name is Danny Thornton. I am a child of God. I am washed by the blood of the Lamb, and my name is written in the Lamb's Book of Life, so look out, devil, you're messing with the wrong man, and get thee behind me in Jesus' name." Make this type of confession quick, and do it often; it does take practice, so never give up!

CONFESSION: I will see me as You see me, Lord!

PRAYER

Father, I refuse to be Satan's POW. I ask You to continue to reveal to me who I am in Christ, for You always cause me to triumph. In Jesus' name, amen.

Day 2: Old Perspectives

> And he said unto him, Oh my Lord, wherewith shall I
> save Israel? behold, my family is poor in Manasseh, and
> I am the least in my father's house. And the Lord said
> unto him, Surely I will be with thee, and thou shalt smite
> the Midianites as one man. (Judges 6:15-16 KJV)

After years of living under the enemy's bondage, Israel developed a POW mentality that was being passed down to the next generation. When people are under oppression for an extended period of time, it's hard for them to see themselves any other way. Something has to happen in them to shift the perspective of how they see themselves.

For example, take the woman with the bloody issue in the gospels. She had that same exact shift. She spent years bleeding and feeling weak, sick, and insignificant. Under the law, she was unclean, and if that wasn't enough, she was impoverished after spending all she had on doctors. But there was a shift in her perspective when she heard about Jesus.

> When she had heard of Jesus, came in the press behind,
> and touched his garment. For she said, If I may touch but
> his clothes, I shall be whole. (Mark 5:27-28 KJV)

This frail little lady who was sick for twelve years saw herself healed! And she was!

When we look back at the children of Israel in Judges chapter six, we see that Gideon started making up excuses to talk himself out what God was telling him to do. Let call excuses for what they really are: lies. Excuses are lies. Get rid of the old perspective you have of yourself and trade it for God's perspective and watch your spirit's response.

- Gideon saw himself as a scared young man, but God saw him as a warrior.

- Moses saw himself as a complete failure, but God saw in him as Israel's Hero.

- David saw himself as a forgotten young shepherd boy, but God saw a king and a prophet.

- Mary saw herself as ordinary, but God saw a supernatural vessel.

- Peter saw himself as a rough fisherman working on the sea; God saw him as a fisher of men.

The moment you see yourself as God sees you, you will begin to sense God's purpose for your life. You will begin to see the potential and the ability God put in you. When you see yourself as God sees you, you will have what I call "Godfidence." Godfidence is when you think clearly, you stand tall and confidently, and your trust is completely in God. That is what happened to Gideon. When he acquired his "Godfidence" is when Gideon responded to the Holy Spirit and did exactly what God had called him to accomplish. When you see yourself as God sees you, God expects a RESPONSE from you, as He expected from Gideon.

So how do you see yourself? What do you do if you don't like the way you see yourself? Be honest and talk to the Holy Spirit, and ask to have His perspective. Practice not comparing yourself to others. Finally, love yourself.

CONFESSION: I am a child of God, I am washed by the blood of the Lamb, and my name is written in the Book of Life. So look out, devil, here comes God's Army!

PRAYER

Father, in the name of Jesus, I cast down the stronghold of low self-esteem that has lied to me for years. I bind that attitude and renounce it in the name of Jesus. Holy Spirit, help me recognize it when it rises up and tries to lie to me again. Lord, protect me from low self-esteem's partner: pride. Do not allow pride to seep into my philosophy and contaminate it. I want to walk and live as Jesus did. With Your help, Lord, it is done!

Day 3: The Fire Must Never Go Out

Remember, the fire must be kept burning on the altar at
all times. It must never go out. (Leviticus 6:13 NLT)

Some years ago, our drama team put on a skit entitled "Campfire,"
and I still remember it to this day. One of the characters was always
instructing everyone about how to keep the campfire burning, while
another character would repeatedly whine out loud, "it's too hard," in a
funny, squeaky voice.

The symbolism of the passage in Leviticus and the Campfire skit is
a vivid truth when you look at it with New Testament eyes. We are to be
the keepers of the fire that God put in us. Paul exhorted his gospel son
in second Timothy 1:6, "This is why I remind you to fan into flames the
spiritual gift God gave you."

What gift was Paul talking about? The gift of the life of God, His
Holy Spirit inside of you. The enemy—your opposer—is doing his best
to quench the fire out in us, and he has thrown many a wet blanket on our
fires. He does it by dousing us with the water of lies, the dirt of our flesh,
and by stomping on us with his feet of temptations and condemnation.

But the Spirit of God within us declares: "No more!" My desire is to
be a "man on fire," and I know you desire to be on fire too.

Satan doesn't have any consequence in quenching the fire; only we
do. Keeping the fire of the Holy Spirit alive in us is our responsibility.
Paul wrote, "Quench not the Spirit" (1 Thessalonians 5:19 KJV). This
wasn't written to Satan but to us. Satan doesn't have the power to quench
the fire in us, so he uses deception—lies to convince us that what he says
is the truth. So when you feel the Holy Spirit nudging you forward to

pray, read the Word, witness, prophesy—or do anything for the Lord—just do it. Every time you don't do as the Holy Spirit leads you to do, your sensitivity to him is dulled. And don't want that to happen. "For as many as are led by the Spirit of God, they are the sons of God" (Romans 8:14 KJV).

Read this very carefully: no one can carry revival into any home, any church, or any city if they do not have personal revival themselves. Has the Holy Spirit asked you to do something recently? If so, have you been saying no to Him? Do you think it is a good idea to say yes? Of course you do; you're a child of God!

Maybe you're asking yourself, "Why am I so spiritually dry?" It's a great start to be open and honest. And I have some good news for you: *the drier you are, the easier it is for you to catch on fire for Jesus*!

CONFESSION: The fire of the Holy Ghost will never go out in me!

PRAYER

Father God, I repent for allowing the fire of God to simmer low. I take full responsibility for this fire. It must never go out, and with Your help, Holy Spirit, It will NEVER GO OUT! Lord, I ask You to keep my heart right before You and the people in my life. I want personal revival to be resident in me.

Let Your fire have its way in me, Lord, to keep the enemy away from my loved ones and me. In Jesus' name, amen.

Day 4: Does Fire Burn?

"Quench not the Spirit." (1 Thessalonians 5:19 KJV)

I heard a story about two men who went hunting in the wild. They were supposed to take turns sleeping to keep the campfire burning. The most experienced hunter slept first, but before he retired to the tent, he instructed his partner not to let the fire go out. Unfortunately, the man neglected to keep the fire going. When the first man couldn't sleep, he came out of the tent in the middle of the night. Just as he was about to comment about the fire going out, the other man said, "Hey, look at the lights out there. It looks like a house far away, and you can see the lights in the windows." The man took one quick look and yelled out, "Quick! Stoke the fire and get out your gun. Those lights are the eyes of wolves moving in!"

There is a reason why God wants us to be on fire. Wolves are on the prowl, and we need to keep the fire burning in our life. This is why the writer of First Thessalonians says not to quench the Spirit. The word *quench* means "to extinguish."[1] We are not to live a life or make decisions that would extinguish the fire of the Spirit in us. Satan's plan is to kill, steal and destroy you, but God's plan is to give you life abundantly. (John 10:10).

So keep putting logs on the fire of your soul—logs of prayer, reading, and studying the Word, and logs of praying in the spirit. Don't neglect the gift of God that is in you. Prophesy when the Spirit gives you the utterance. Be bold and be strong, for the Lord your God is with you. Most importantly, give your life as a log to the Lord. Give Him something to work with.

What does fire do? It purifies, cleanses, changes appearances of things, raises the temperature, gives light to those around it, and it attracts.

---

1. Webster's Collegiate Dictionary, s.v. "quench," (G & C Merriam, Co: Springfield, MA, 1913).

Notice that I didn't say that fire burns. Fire doesn't just burn by itself. It needs something to combust with. To say a building is burning is correct because fire needs something that will burn. When God sends His fire, He sends it when He finds someone who is willing to be consumed by Him.

Remember the story of the burning bush?

> And the angel of the Lord appeared unto him in a flame of fire out of the midst of a bush: and he looked, and, behold, the bush burned with fire, and the bush was not consumed. (Exodus 3:2 KJV)

The fire of God is not destructible, so you don't have to be afraid of it. I would be concerned if I wasn't on fire. I want to catch on fire!

I believe if Jesus drank coffee at a coffee shop, He would order it hot:

> So then because thou art lukewarm, and neither cold nor hot, I will spue thee out of my mouth. (Revelation 3:16 KJV)

Ask yourself these questions:

- Does Jesus want you on fire?
- Are you fanning the flame of the Spirit in you?
- Are you giving God something to work with?
- If not? Why not?

If you are fanning the flame, then you are combustible. To be combustible means you're capable of catching on fire. Offer yourself up to Jesus, as the saying goes: no sacrifice, no fire.

CONFESSION: Set me on fire, Lord; set me on fire!

PRAYER

Lord, I know that wolves surround me. I cannot see them, and I plan on keeping it that way. With Your help, Holy Spirit, I will continue to lay log after log in my life to keep me burning for You. In Jesus' name, amen!

Day 5: John the Baptist Wasn't a Balanced Guy

John's clothes were woven from coarse camel hair, and he wore a leather belt around his waist. For food he ate locusts and wild honey. People from Jerusalem and from all of Judea and all over the Jordan Valley went out to see and hear John. And when they confessed their sins, he baptized them in the Jordan River. (Matthew 3:4-6 NLT)

From the passage above, you can tell that John the Baptist was not a balanced guy. I would also like to point out that Jesus wasn't either. Look at something that Jesus said,

Then Jesus said unto them, Verily, verily, I say unto you, Except ye eat the flesh of the Son of man, and drink his blood, ye have no life in you. (John 6:53 KJV)

That was highly unusual for someone to say that. We know now, Jesus was speaking spiritually, not naturally. That is why he lost so many followers that day.

I am aware that someone who's emotionally or mentally unstable could take what I am saying here and run the wrong way with it. I am not responsible for that. My goal is to stir up the gift of God inside you and inspire you to rebel against the spirit of the world by living a life of obedience to God.

Answer these questions:

- Do you consider yourself radical for God?
- Are you living a mediocre Christian life?

SOAR IN HIS STRENGTH

- If so, how long are you going to live a mediocre Christian life?
- Do you think that there might be more to Christianity than what you have experienced?

Some of you reading this understand what I am saying. Others who do not may be thinking, "Oh, he's being judgmental." Well, you are free to think what you want, but I refuse to settle for being ordinary when God put extraordinary inside of me—and it is the same for you, believer. I would be incapable of releasing the joy that God has intended for me to release. Unreleased joy creates constipated Christians.

Do you sense the Holy Spirit speaking to you to go to another level in your walk with God? Do you need help breaking out of the norm and need some guidance? Let me help you go from an ordinary life to an extraordinary life. You can begin right here in the Word of God:

> Don't copy the behavior and customs of this world, but let God transform you into a new person by changing the way you think. Then you will learn to know God's will for you, which is good and pleasing and perfect. (Romans 12:2 NLT)

If you ask the Holy Spirit to help fulfill this passage of scripture, get ready to be called a radical. And when they do, you can rejoice because it will be proof that you are being transformed to live in the extraordinary!

CONFESSION: I want to life the extraordinary life to which You called me!

PRAYER

Thank You, Jesus. I want to be sold out and radical. I do not want to be a friend to this carnal world. I want to be separated from its philosophy. I am not called to be weird; I am called to be a friend of God. In Jesus' name, amen.

Day 6: Persecution Will Follow

Blessed are ye, when men shall revile you, and persecute you, and shall say all manner of evil against you falsely, for my sake. Rejoice, and be exceeding glad: for great is your reward in heaven: for so persecuted they the prophets which were before you. (Matthew 5:11-12 KJV)

When I mention being radical, I'm talking about being an on-fire Christian. We are told to be "in the world but not of it," but still have to live every day here on earth among many lost people. In the process, we need to make sure we do not compromise our walk with God, so we remain effective in reaching people with the gospel. As radical as John the Baptist was, people still flocked to hear his message. He found his balance in the calling and Word of God. Jesus said this about him:

I tell you the truth, of all who have ever lived, none is greater than John the Baptist. Yet even the least person in the kingdom of heaven is greater than he is! (Matthew 11:11 NLT)

When you put both hands on the plow and don't look back, you can open the door to the most extraordinary and exciting life a human could ever live. That's an on-fire, Bible-loving, tongue-talking, radical Christian life. Is that too much for you?

Let's look at something else Jesus said:

Then Jesus said to his disciples, "If any of you wants to be my follower, you must give up your own way, take up your cross, and follow me. If you try to hang on to your life, you will lose it. But if you give up your life for my sake, you will save it. (Matthew 16:24-25 NLT)

Being a Christian and a radical to the world can cost you your family, friends, and sometimes even your job. Of course, the world will mock you and persecute you, but be of good cheer!

Being radical is more normal than you may think. Being radical is:

- Being the best employee your company has
- Arriving at your job early and starting when the bell rings
- Paying your employees a living wage
- Loving your wife like Christ loves the church
- Tithing to your house of worship
- Attending your house of worship
- Praying for your president, prime minister, or those in authority—even if you don't like them

Is that too radical for you? If it is, you have some issues to take up with God.

CONFESSION: I'm not going to live an ordinary life; I'm going to live an EXTRAORDINARY LIFE!

PRAYER

Jesus, I want to be like You, Lord. I want the Bible to come alive to me. I want the deaf to see, the lame to walk, and the eyes of the blind to be opened through my life. I know it starts with me. I give You my heart; I give You my life. With Your power, I will not conform to this world's customs but be an example of kingdom living. Thank You, Lord. Amen.

Day 7: Barroom Brawl

Then they spat on his face and slapped him. Others struck
him over and over with their fists. (Matthew 26:67 TPT)

When I read the Bible, I usually try to put myself into the story, into
the very room or environment that the writer is conveying. One
day as I was reading, I came to the above scripture.

I'm sure the room was filled with male testosterone. But unfortunately, there was also the presence of evil, the smell of blood and death,
cruelty, and much, much more. One way to describe it (and, trust me, it
comes short of it), is as if you are in the middle of a barroom brawl with
Hell's Angels Motorcycle Club, and your family was with you, and you
realize that there's no way to get out. Again, the presence of evil was in
the room, and it was thick with anger, murder, and hatred—and Jesus
was trapped there. If that wasn't enough, He had the mental agony of
knowing that it was going to get worse.

I cannot pull my imagination away from that ruthless, horrible
room where our gentle Jesus, the Lamb of God, was. The Bible goes
on and says:

And they stripped him, and put on him a scarlet robe.
And when they had platted a crown of thorns, they put
it upon his head, and a reed in his right hand: and they
bowed the knee before him, and mocked him, saying,
Hail, King of the Jews! And they spit upon him, and took
the reed, and smote him on the head. And after that they
had mocked him, they took the robe off from him, and

put his own raiment on him, and led him away to crucify him. (Matthew 27:28-31 KJV)

How humiliating, painful, hurtful, and agonizing it must have been for our Jesus! How evil, horrible, nauseating, and sick the whole scene was. Let me ask you a few questions:

- Do you believe in evil spirits?

- Do you believe in the demonic?

- What thoughts come to you about the suffering Jesus was experiencing?

- If you were in the room, do you think you would have the courage to say, "Hey, leave my Jesus alone!"

That room was filled with pure evil and demonic presence—and mankind took part in it. Chances are, if you were one of Jesus' disciples, you would have fled like the rest of them. The men who did this to Him were Roman soldiers. A Roman soldier recruit had to be seventeen years of age and had to be a Roman citizen. Every recruit had to be fit for fighting; no weaklings or short men could be a Roman Soldier, and when they enlisted, it was for at least twenty-five years of service. These were the macho men of that era.

But the one who would be judged worst was the man who betrayed Jesus: Judas. That betrayal was the epitome of those who will be sent to hell. So how can I end this devotional on the bright side? Remember this: HE DID ALL OF THIS FOR YOU.

CONFESSION: Thank You, Lord, You did it for me!

PRAYER

Jesus, I want to believe that I would rescue You from that evil, but that would not be unreasonable. All men have sinned and come short of the glory of God. But because You died, were buried, and rose from the dead, I can live. Thank You, Lord! In Jesus' name, amen.

Day 8: Not Even a Sliver Of Evil

And he cast down the pieces of silver in the temple, and departed, and went and hanged himself. (Matthew 27:5 KJV)

When I read Judas' story of how he betrayed the Lord, I don't know if he really thought they would actually kill Jesus. Maybe that's why when he found out Jesus was condemned to death, he couldn't take it anymore. His betrayal got the best of him. The evil that Judas succumbed to was no different than the evil that was in that room with Jesus. Those spirits began to torment him mercilessly. And the only way Judas believed he could get out of this torment was to kill himself.

I relate to folks who had to deal with suicidal thoughts. There was a season in my life when I attempted suicide three times. I like to keep the first two attempts to myself; only my wife and maybe a few close friends know about those, which were definitely a cry for help. But the last attempt to end my life was very serious.

I was in my car driving home one morning at about 3 a.m. I was distraught because I was sick of how I was living my life. I thought the only way out of it was to kill myself. As I started driving home, I was thinking to myself, "How can I kill myself?" Then a thought came to me, and for some reason, I spoke it out loud; I said, "I know how I am going to kill myself, I'll let myself go crazy." I repeated, "I'll let myself go crazy," about a hundred times non-stop, and got louder by the minute. Pretty crazy, huh? Then it got worse. I slammed my foot on the accelerator and didn't hold anything back on my Pontiac Grande Ville, moving fast toward a brick wall.

Suddenly the car was filled with an evil presence. In my heart, I knew it was an evil spirit that was there to do me harm and take me to a place I didn't want to go. My car door opened, and I heard a deep, dark voice in my right ear say, "JUMP!" I was terrified and yelled out, "No!" and shut the door. At the time, I was Catholic, but I still knew where to go when I needed help fast. I screamed at the top of my lungs, "JESUS, JESUS, JESUS!"

The evil presence left the car instantly, and Jesus showed up and delivered me. This encounter ignited my search for truth, and I found Jesus—or rather, Jesus found me!

That evil presence left after I called out Jesus' name, and I was shaking uncontrollably and desperately trying to regain my composure as I sat in my car. What strikes me is that the evil I felt wasn't even a sliver of the intense evil that Jesus felt that dreaded day when he was arrested. I am reminded of this scripture when I think of that day I was trying to kill myself.

> But everyone who calls on the name of the Lord will be saved. (Acts 2:21 NLT)

Please do not wait until you are suicidal to give your heart and life to God. Jesus said: "Come unto me, all ye that labour and are heavy laden, and I will give you rest" (Matthew 11:28 KJV).

DECLARATION: I will fear no evil!

PRAYER

Father God, You are almighty, powerful, and omnipotent. You know where I'm at today. I may be suicidal or ready to give up on myself, my marriage, my ministry, or whatever—but if I call on Your name, You will save me. In Jesus' name, amen.

Day 9: The Great Deception

When he speaketh a lie, he speaketh of his own: for he is
a liar, and the father of it. (John 8:44 KJV)

It is not just big lies that are wrong, but what people call "small lies" or "white lies" are wrong too. Satan uses small, little white lies to convince people that if they turn their lives over to God, their life will come to an end. In other words, he tries to convince them that God will take all the fun and excitement out of your life. Remember, the devil is not just a liar, but rather he is the father of lies.

After my encounter with God and the sliver of evil in my car, I began my search for truth. It's so amazing how God will lead you if you are sincere. God will always lead and guide those who love truth. At the beginning of my search, the Holy Spirit intervened and stopped me from making connections with certain individuals. I found out a few years later that one particular individual I had been trying to connect to was the president of a psychic group in my community. That, my friend, would have led me in a very wrong direction because I was not grounded in the Word of truth yet.

Then I made a second connection with a godly couple named Glenn and Carrol Johnson, who also lived near my community. During our first encounter, my wife was very apprehensive. I understood; I was too. It was 1978: the same year that Jim Jones and his nine hundred followers committed mass suicide in Cape Town, South Africa.

I purposely met this couple at their house because I didn't want to kick them out of our house (which I had done a couple of times already). We went to their home with eyes wide open with caution. I noticed that the outside of their home was neat and clean, and when we went inside, it was clean, carpeted, and quite homey. As we sat and talked in the Johnson's living room, we asked them many questions. I'd had several conversations with them on the phone, but my wife had not communicated with them at all before that day. As we were talking, my wife asked, "What do Christians do to have fun? Go to miniature golf or bowling?" I thought it was funny, and it seemed true. But that was the great deception. The enemy tries to make you believe if you turn your life over to God, He will take all the fun and excitement out of your life, and it will be very dull.

Well, guess what? He's a *liar*! Answer these questions below:

- What lies has satan told you?
- Have you believed the lie that becoming a Christian will make your life boring?
- How is your life now, after Christ?
- Are you ready for God's truth?

If you come to God wholeheartedly, you will come to realize that the great deception held you back. Living wholeheartedly for God is the most exciting life a human can ever live. And the good news is that we will continue to live—even after we leave this planet. You will enjoy *eternal life*!

CONFESSION: I have a love for the truth!

PRAYER

Thank You, Jesus, for everything You have done for me. Thank You for giving me the love of the truth, which feeds me more and more truth. In Jesus' name, amen.

Day 10: Come On, Follow Me

Be ye followers of me, even as I also am of Christ.
(1 Corinthians 11:1 KJV)

I used to work at a top-40 radio station, and in nightclubs with light shows, fog machines, infinity boxes, lighted dance floors, laser lights, dancing competitions, and I even got to sign autographs. I loved the DJ lifestyle! Why? I love to dance to disco music; I love playing records and mixing them and creating new music, and of course, I liked all of the attention. But when Jesus got my attention, my head and heart turned toward Him. That's when I walked away from the nightlife because I knew the Holy Spirit was leading me out of it. I didn't know what to expect, but I knew I had to obey God. I loved my job so much that I wept that last night when I left. But it didn't change my mind because my heart was fixed on Jesus, and I knew I had to die to this world.

I'm not saying you have to leave your job when you get saved. I knew that I had to leave mine. It was similar to what the Bible said about Abraham's nephew Lot, "(For that righteous man dwelling among them, in seeing and hearing, vexed his righteous soul from day to day with their unlawful deeds;)." (2 Peter 2:8 KJV). The nightclub scene was vexing my righteous soul and causing havoc to my marriage.

When I left the nightlife, I was left alone and was quite disappointed. I wondered how people could not want Jesus? I thought. I invited many of my co-workers and friends to come follow me. They looked at me like I was weird. "Oh, you found the light," some would say. I was able to share my testimony with all of them, including my boss, and they thought it was brilliant, but they didn't want to leave Sodom and Gomorrah.

Things began to change when I stepped out and obeyed God. Reading the Word became exciting, fellowshipping with my brothers and sisters was stimulating, and going to church to worship and hear the Word preached was thrilling. It was God's Spirit in me that changed everything. I was and am still enthusiastic about the things of God and the hobbies, talents, and gifts God put in me.

All I wanted them to do was follow me to Jesus. How about your friends? Have you told your friends about Jesus? Have you shared your testimony with them?

Please don't allow condemnation to come on you as you read this. Just be willing and open to witness to someone today. I always have liked the story of Matthew, the tax collector, leaving his job to follow Jesus.

> As Jesus was walking along, he saw a man named Matthew sitting at his tax collector's booth. "Follow me and be my disciple," Jesus said to him. So Matthew got up and followed him. (Matthew 9:9 NLT)

See that, no drama! He simply got up and followed Jesus. Brilliant!

CONFESSION: I am not ashamed of the gospel of Jesus Christ!

PRAYER

Father, I face another day at the office, the factory, the hospital, or university. Some days are very tough, but I know You are with me. "For God has said, "I will never fail you. I will never abandon you" (Hebrews 13:5 NLT)

You are the great Promise Keeper, and I love You. Lord, I know You are in me, and I ask You to help me love You with all of my heart, soul, mind, and strength. I know that's the secret to experiencing the exciting Christian life! Thank You, Jesus. Amen.

Day 11: Your Dominant Thought Will Dominate

The thoughts of the [steadily] diligent tend only to plenteousness. (Proverbs 21:5 AMPC)

Allow me to put this scripture in my words:

> The thoughts of people who tend to be industrious, busy, and engaged in what God called them to do will produce plenty in their life.

People who are moving in faith, moving in the things of God, and engaged in fulfilling the vision God gave them will be filled with thoughts of what God called them to do. The result is that they will have plenty because they are pleasing God. The Bible tells us that without faith, it is impossible to please Him (Hebrews 11:6).

You need to train your thought life to be connected, tapped into, and yielded to the mind of Christ God gave you on a daily basis. God will never give you thoughts that are negative, lustful, or of failure; those come from the enemy. But if you are seeking God wholeheartedly, He will honor your time with Him and give you His strategy for your life.

> For I know the plans I have for you," declares the Lord, "plans to prosper you and not to harm you, plans to give you hope and a future. Then you will call on me and come and pray to me, and I will listen to you. You will seek me and find me when you seek me with all your heart. (Jeremiah 29:11-13 NIV)

Consider this: the direction of your life is dictated by your thoughts. If you don't like the direction of your life, then you need to change your thought process. You will always move in the direction of your dominant thought!

When you read the Word, read it with the mindset that you have a right to every promise in the Bible. Not because you deserve it but because He earned it. Fill your mind with His thoughts, His ways, and His plan—and watch the direction of your life shift toward His promises like tectonic plates shift on the earth. You cannot afford to think any other way!

This is why the apostle wrote this:

> Do not conform to the pattern of this world, but be transformed by the renewing of your mind. Then you will be able to test and approve what God's will is—his good, pleasing and perfect will. (Romans 12:2 NIV)

Renewing your mind is a cleansing process where you eliminate the thoughts and philosophy that do not line up with God's philosophy. You were contaminated by the world. The way you were raised, the parents you had, the teachers or professors who taught you, and your friends all have had a profound effect on you. Even the church you attend is an essential key for getting worldliness out of your mind and putting the Word of God into your heart. Some might call this being brainwashed if they do not know the Lord, but the truth is that we are blood-washed by the blood of the Lamb.

CONFESSION: I will think the way God wants me to think!

PRAYER

Father, help me see myself the way You see me. Allow me to believe that I am in Christ and that You are well pleased with me. Lord, I pray for a shift in my old thinking to kingdom thinking. With the Holy Spirit helping me, I can and will do this. Thank You for hearing my prayer. Today is going to be a good day! In Jesus' name, amen.

Day 12: The Holy Ghost Check

Now therefore, thus says the Lord of hosts, "Consider your ways and thoughtfully reflect on your conduct! (Haggai 1:5 AMP)

We have a responsibility to work out our salvation. Not earn it, but walk/work out what God put in us. There are times when we must pause and reflect on how we have been behaving: the way we have been treating our spouse, children, friends, or co-workers. I like to say that we need a check-up from the neck up!

There are not too many times in our life when we can claim to be ignorant of our sinful ways. That's because we have someone living on the inside of us who will remind us when our conduct isn't lining up with His Word. It's called the Holy Ghost Check. No, it's not a new dance; it's how God ushers His grace toward us and helps us learn to walk in the Spirit.

And grieve not the holy Spirit of God, whereby ye are sealed unto the day of redemption. (Ephesians 4:30 KJV)

To *grieve* means to be distressed, to be sad, cause grief, be in heaviness, sorrowful.[2]

How does the Holy Ghost Check work? It's easy! When you say or do something, and you have a grieving feeling on this inside of you, that's the Holy Ghost Check telling you that you've just said or done something that has made Him sad, and He doesn't want you to do that

2. "G3076 - lypeō - Strong's Greek Lexicon (KJV)." Blue Letter Bible. Accessed 3 May, 2021. https://www.blueletterbible.org//lang/lexicon/lexicon.cfm?Strongs=G3076&t=KJV.

anymore. Even though God has forgiven you of all of your sins, it still grieves the Holy Spirit.

What you do next is very important. To explain this, I would like to illustrate my relationship between my wife and myself. As I am writing this, we have been married for forty-nine years, so I have some experience! If I do or say something that troubles my wife, and she points it out, our relationship will suffer if I ignore it or shrug it off. If I keep ignoring her complaint, our relationship would be hindered. We will be married and in love with each other, but we will not be "one" with each other like we use to be. But if I apologize and acknowledge my wrong to her, and then reflect on my ways and behavior and work on them, we will embrace each other and continue doing kingdom business.

If you haven't read the verse below, it is an eye-opener for husbands:

> In the same way, you husbands must give honor to your wives. Treat your wife with understanding as you live together. She may be weaker than you are, but she is your equal partner in God's gift of new life. **Treat her as you should so your prayers will not be hindered.** (1 Peter 3:7 NLT)

Answer the following questions:

- If you are married, has the Holy Spirit given you a check about how you treat your bride?
- Have you ever had that Holy Ghost Check toward anyone?
- How did you respond to Him?
- Have you ever had to say you're sorry to someone after that Holy Ghost Check?

Remember, God does not give you these feelings randomly. The Holy Spirit loves you, and He is inspiring you to be all you can be in Christ!

CONFESSION: The Holy Ghost Check is my heart-rate monitor!

PRAYER

Father, I thank You for the Holy Spirit. Holy Spirit, Your love for me is evident by the way You lovingly deal with me. Help me remain sensitive to You. In Jesus' name, amen.

Day 13: Does God Have a Plan for My Life?

"For I know the plans I have for you," declares the Lord, "plans to prosper you and not to harm you, plans to give you hope and a future." (Jeremiah 29:11 NIV)

Yes, God has a plan for your life. He doesn't just have "the plan," He also knows the strategy for you to accomplish the plan. If you believe that, then you would do what the next verse says:

Then you will call on me and come and pray to me. (Jeremiah 29:12 NIV)

When you know God has a plan for you, you will seek Him whole-heartedly. Please note: half-heartedness doesn't make the cut with God. Wholeheartedness will always get God's attention. And when God speaks to you, it will prepare you for the future. That's what prayer is about: the future. Everything you pray for is something you want to have or to see done in the future.

There is another aspect that is crucial for us to be able to hear from God to learn His strategy for our future, and that is having the joy of the Lord in our lives.

My brethren, count it all joy when ye fall into divers temptations. (James 1:2 KJV)

Paul instructs us to maintain the joy of the Lord when we find ourselves in the midst of temptations or multiple troubles. Joy ushers strength into our souls and creates a healthy environment. This healthy environment helps us hear the voice of God. Fear, anxiety, depression, or anger in the midst of your troubles is not conducive to hearing the wisdom of God, so counter it with joy!

Now we find that the best strategy for doing this is by gaining wisdom from God.

> If any of you lack wisdom, let him ask of God, that giveth to all men liberally, and upbraideth not; and it shall be given him. (James 1:5 KJV)

The term *strategy* is used to indicate a plan of action designed to achieve a major or overall aim. The wisdom of God will help lead you by giving you a step-by-step action plan to lead you through the temptations and troubles you're going through. Wisdom is the vehicle that will guide, lead, and inspire you in the midst of troubles, and the joy of the Lord will give you the strength to endure anything that comes your way.

Answer these questions:

- Are you in the midst of trouble?
- Have you asked God for His wisdom?
- What is God speaking to you concerning your life?
- What was the last thing God spoke to you about?
- Have you done what He asked you to do?
- If not, why not?

I encourage you today to ask God for the wisdom to soar above the obstacles you are facing.

CONFESSION: I have been created to soar in life!

PRAYER

Lord, when I sense trouble coming, I will train myself to go to You and ask for Your wisdom. Until I do, I will maintain the joy of the Lord to create a healthy environment to hear the Word of the Lord and His strategy for my life. In Jesus' name, amen.

Day 14: So What Is God Saying to You?

Then the Lord called out again, "Samuel!" Again Samuel got up and went to Eli. "Here I am. Did you call me?" "I didn't call you, my son," Eli said. "Go back to bed." Samuel did not yet know the Lord because he had never had a message from the Lord before. So the Lord called a third time, and once more Samuel got up and went to Eli. "Here I am. Did you call me?" Then Eli realized it was the Lord who was calling the boy. So he said to Samuel, "Go and lie down again, and if someone calls again, say, 'Speak, Lord, your servant is listening.'" So Samuel went back to bed. (1 Samuel 3:6-9 NLT)

I asked my grandson a few years ago, "So what is God saying to you?" He looked at me with a bewildered face like he swallowed a fly and said, "Huh?" I thought his reaction was funny, but nevertheless, God speaks to children, teenagers, young people, and even elderly people. We have to challenge not just ourselves but also our loved ones to hear from God. Samuel was a little guy when the Lord captured his attention. God woke him up three times in one night, and Samuel went to Eli because He wasn't used to hearing the voice of the Lord. After the third time that sacred night, Eli had enough sense to recognize that the Lord was speaking to this young boy. (keep in mind this is the Old Testament, and God spoke audibly to His people)

Now the big question is: what is God saying to you:

- About your life?
- About your future?
- About your children?

- About the college or university to go to?
- About your career or calling?

If you don't know what the Holy Spirit is speaking to you about, you will have a difficult time leading even yourself, let alone others under your leadership, business, or home.

> If you need wisdom, ask our generous God, and he will give it to you. He will not rebuke you for asking. But when you ask him, be sure that your faith is in God alone. Do not waver, for a person with divided loyalty is as unsettled as a wave of the sea that is blown and tossed by the wind. (James 1:5-6 NLT)

When God speaks to you, it will always be in the form of "wisdom." How can I say that? Because God has never said a stupid thing. Life is not a riddle but rather a puzzle. God isn't trying to chide you or trick you. What He speaks to you will be a piece of the puzzle of your life. Then you need the faith and courage to apply that wisdom to your life. Doing so will help guide you to your destination and the fulfillment of your assignment here on earth. So do you need wisdom? Ask God!

DECLARATION: Father, I receive Your wisdom by faith!

PRAYER

Father, I believe You have a plan for me. I ask that You speak to me through impressions, the Word of God, and in my prayer time. I ask for the wisdom and the strategy that I need to fulfill my destiny. I also ask You for the faith and courage to use the wisdom You give me. In Jesus' name, amen.

Day 15: My Dream Is Too Big for Me. "Exactly!"

This is the word of the Lord unto Zerubbabel, saying, Not by might, nor by power, but by my spirit, saith the Lord of hosts. (Zechariah 4:6 KJV)

I love this passage of scripture because I see it as an emotional stabilizer. God's dream can become overwhelming if we look at it from our human perspective. God's dream is designed to be bigger than you, bigger than your thinking, and bigger than your financial capabilities. Is your dream too big for you? That's exactly the way God designed it! Why? Because it will cause you to place your faith in Him, and when it comes to pass, everyone will know that it was not you who accomplished it, but God.

Zerubbabel was taken back—and possibly a little bewildered—by the vastness of the responsibility of the call of God on his life. So God sent him a prophet to encourage him. The prophet didn't say exactly what I just wrote, but he cut to the chase with calculated, cutting words.

The words of the prophet answered the unasked question in Zerubbabel's mind: "How am I going to do this?" Well, it wasn't going to be done by anything Zerubbabel was capable of doing, that's for sure. Look at how the New Living Translation puts this passage: "It is not by force nor by strength, but by my Spirit, says the Lord of Heaven's Armies."

This scripture stabilizes me by bringing me comfort and peace, knowing that God's got my back. God will back me emotionally, financially, and spiritually as I walk in faith in the direction He has called me to do.

Even though God gives you a big dream, He will only ask you to take a small step toward it. Walking in faith is not a shot in the dark, rather a shot in the light. He will give you the steps to take. It may be making a phone call, sending out resumés, or physically going someplace. It's a step of faith in the right direction, even if it's a very small step, for God will honor it.

> Do not despise these small beginnings, for the Lord rejoices to see the work begin, to see the plumb line in Zerubbabel's hand. (Zechariah 4:10 NLT)

The plumb line is a building instrument that construction workers in that time period used. It is our modern-day it's called a level. You know that two-to-six-foot stick with a bubble in the middle. Do not despise the small steps, for the Lord sees it as you measuring and trying to keep your balance as you walk on water.

CONFESSION: I will be strong and of good courage!

PRAYER

Thank You, Lord, that I can see what you want to be done through me with Your eyes. Your Word says if I seek Your kingdom and righteousness first, all these things will be added to my life. You will provide for me. Lord, I believe that when You give a vision to Your people, You will always provide the PROvision. Thank You, Lord, I receive it in Jesus' name, amen.

Day 16: A Tough Choice Is Still a Choice!

For this day is holy unto our Lord: neither be ye sorry; for
the joy of the Lord is your strength. (Nehemiah 8:10 KJV)

I'm not sure how your day is going so far or what you're facing, but I would like to remind you that *joy is a choice!*

One day I wasn't feeling very joyful, not feeling like the good-natured person I usually am (although I am not a morning person). My fleshly thoughts were stronger than my yielding to godly thoughts. Emotionally, I was having a miserable day.

And you know what? I wasn't going to let it go either. I was planning to make sure everyone around me knew how bad of a day I was having. As I was driving to the office, I allowed one negative thought after another to fill my mind. I was making a very strong case in the Emotional Court of Law in my soul—myself on one side and the Fruit of the Spirit on the other.

There was quite a debate going on in my head when suddenly a strong objection was made from across the courtroom. My thought process came to a screeching halt as my conscience reminded me of a statement: joy is a choice. It was something I had written in my book, *The 9 Spiritual Fronts*. Immediately I got angry with myself, and I begin to reason within myself the validity of that statement. I thought, "Well, maybe I was wrong about that; it can't apply to every situation." I argued internally.

Nevertheless, I continued to think about it, pondered it, and then made a choice.

I decided to yield to the fruit of joy that God put in my born-again spirit. Then I opened my mouth and spoke out loud (yes, I was talking to myself in the car), and I said, "This is a good day, I can do all things through Christ Jesus. God always causes me to triumph in Christ Jesus." By doing this, I spiritually flicked a switch, and the joy of the Lord transferred the GodStrength necessary for me to get through the day!

A few things to note:

- Human happiness depends on what is happening around you
- God's joy is released no matter what is happening around you

That's because:

- Happiness rides on the back of circumstances
- Joy rides on the back of the Word of God

Joy is kingdom steroids!

CONFESSION: I will yield to the joy of the Lord and have a good day!

PRAYER

Jesus, thank You for empowering me with your character. I know that my flesh is weak, but my born-again spirit is always ready to do the will of God. I ask You, Holy Spirit, to remind me with Your loving touch and gentle nudge before I say or do something contrary to how I should behave. Thank You for loving and caring for me. Thank You for the joy of the Lord, for it is truly GodStrength in me and for me.

Day 17: Victorious Over Worry, Part 1

Be careful for nothing; but in every thing by prayer and supplication with thanksgiving let your requests be made known unto God. (Philippians 4:6 KJV)

The NIV says, "Do not be anxious about anything." This may take a couple of days to unpack this truth, but allow me to give you an up-front answer to the question above. I do not believe worrying is a sin that will send you to hell; however, if you continue to worry, it can make your world a living hell.

Everybody gets anxious once in a while—some more than others. Before I go any further, I would like to add a disclaimer: We all experience certain seasons in our lives. It's not always "springtime" in people's lives but instead, deep winter. People have to deal with disappointments, discouragement, and even depression. Sometimes it is a physical thing. I'm not saying to ignore it or not fight the good fight of faith, but sometimes you need to consider professional medical help. I have known people who, for a season, have been on medications. Whether it was due to personal trauma in their life or physical causes, they went on medicine, and then as they got stronger, they went off it.

In my opinion, we should always approach any infirmity as spiritual warfare. So let's look deeper into this.

To sin means to miss the mark. When we worry, we miss the mark of God's Word, which is why Paul instructed us to be careful or anxious for nothing. *Careful* means to be full of care. We are supposed to live by faith, not be full of care. We have to cast the thought of worry down as soon as possible. If we don't, it can take root in your thought life and become a stronghold.

The verse says, "Be full of care for nothing." Nothing means "no thing." I am sure you know what *no thing* means. For example, you purchase something and pay the bill. Now, if a store associate comes to you and says, "Excuse me, but I need to speak to you for a couple of hours concerning what you owe on your purchase. You would say, "No way! I owe you NO-THING." You can use this same approach when worry comes to fill your mind with anxiety. You need to say, "No! Get out of here. I owe you nothing. My mind belongs to Jesus Christ and will live my life by faith, not by sight or care."

This takes practice. Yes, you have to practice Christianity in all of its facets. After all, doctors practice medicine on you, and even lawyers practice law. Likewise, we must practice living by faith. If we are filled with the cares of this world, it will deplete the GodStrength in us, and we will lose our peace.

When we lose our peace, we can lose our focus, and the enemy can come in like a flood. But be of good cheer; God will raise up a standard if you will only believe.

CONFESSION: I declare in Jesus' name that I will not worry anymore!

PRAYER

Jesus, my Prince of Peace, I ask You to come and comfort me during this time. I know You will comfort me, and ministry will be birthed in me so I can comfort those the same way You have comforted me through trying times. Father, I ask You to usher Your presence into my mind, my thought life. I ask You to remind me to raise up the standard of Your Word and use the authority You have given me as a believer. In Jesus' name, amen.

Day 18: Victorious Over Worry, Part 2

Be careful for nothing; but in everything by prayer and supplication with thanksgiving let your requests be made known unto God. (Philippians 4:6 KJV)

I don't know if you noticed it, but within this passage is something we can practice to consistently cast worry out of our mind and be VICTORIOUS OVER WORRY.

Keep in mind that it was the Apostle Paul who wrote this epistle. Let me share with you just a little of what he has gone through:

Five times I received from the Jews the forty lashes minus one. Three times I was beaten with rods, once I was pelted with stones, three times I was shipwrecked, I spent a night and a day in the open sea, I have been constantly on the move. I have been in danger from rivers, in danger from bandits, in danger from my fellow Jews, in danger from Gentiles; in danger in the city, in danger in the country, in danger at sea; and in danger from false believers. I have labored and toiled and have often gone without sleep; I have known hunger and thirst and have often gone without food; I have been cold and naked. Besides everything else, I face daily the pressure of my concern for all the churches. (2 Corinthians 11:24-28 NIV)

Paul gives us insight into how he got through all of this, "But in everything by prayer and supplication with thanksgiving, I made my requests known unto God."

For example, while Paul was floating out in the deep sea on a log or something, he was casting every worry out of his mind, he made his request made known to God—*and here's the clincher*—he did it with thanksgiving!

He protected his mind and heart by attaching thanksgiving to his requests to God. I have never known of a man besides Jesus Christ who has suffered so much for the advancement of the kingdom of God. Look at this: "And herein do I exercise myself, to have always a conscience void of offense toward God, and toward men" (Acts 24:16 KJV).

If you are unthankful or ungrateful, you could develop resentment toward man or even God.

The King James Version says *exercise*, and in Greek, it means "to train." He trained himself, or in other words, you could say he practiced this. Now it's your turn; you have all day to work out at God's Gym for the transfer of GodStrength.

CONFESSION: I am going to thank God today—no matter what!

PRAYER

Father, first, I want to repent of all my murmuring and complaining and for not being grateful and thankful for all that You have done for me. I have some difficult things in my life that I am facing, and I want to thank You in advance for working on behalf of me, my family, and my loved ones. I know that all things work together for good to those who love You, to those who are called according to Your purpose. I will keep my mind care-free and filled with the peace of God and my heart filled with thanksgiving today. In Jesus' name, amen.

Day 19: The Fear of the Lord Is Not Terror of the Lord

Those who fear the Lord are secure; he will be a refuge for their children. (Proverbs 14:26 NLT)

The verse above shows another commandment with a promise attached to it. But to fully grasp this proverb, please understand that the word *fear* in Hebrew means "to revere or reverence."[3] It doesn't mean that we should be terrified of God.

Some of you reading this may remember years ago way, way back (being humorous) when we were instructed to address the parents of our friends at school like this, "Hello, Mr. and Mrs. So and So."

By doing that, we showed reverence to an older generation. I don't know exactly when this stopped, but it seems to have been replaced by calling older people by their first name. Is it wrong? I'm not sure; I can only speak from my own experience. My younger daughter's friends would either just say hi or hello, or some would call me Danny. But one of her friends (who happened to be a bit on the wild side but was very likable) would always greet me by saying, "Hello, Mr. Thornton." It made me feel good!

The late great Ms. Aretha Franklin brought a word to the forefront of our thinking when she sang about it in her song "Respect. " (I'm sure you are singing it now.) We should always show respect and reverence to everyone. You may not respect someone, but that doesn't give you a license to disrespect anyone.

---

3. "H3374 - yir'â - Strong's Hebrew Lexicon (KJV)." Blue Letter Bible. Accessed 3 May, 2021. https://www.blueletterbible.org//lang/lexicon/lexicon.cfm?Strongs=H3374&t=KJV.

Consider this today. The passage says that those who fear (reverence, respect) the Lord God will be a refuge for their children.

As parents and grandparents who reverence the Lord, we are thankful that God has blessed us to have a place to call home for my children and grandchildren, but more importantly, they have found that as they *reverence* the Lord, they have a place in Him and that He will never leave them nor forsake them.

Consider the extreme opposite of this in the condition of the ways of the world. It is impossible for me to list all the horrible acts around us and our cities and countries. Why are all these things happening? Why are there so many shootings, killings, and disrespect for our law enforcement? What makes a 14-year-old child shoot someone in the head with a gun and then eat lunch at a burger joint minutes later like nothing ever happened. They have no conscience or remorse and no reflection on their behavior—they even brag about it.

I will tell you why this is happening: THEY HAVE NO FEAR OF THE LORD!

> And unto man he said, Behold, the fear of the Lord, that is wisdom; and to depart from evil is understanding. (Job 28:28 KJV)

The wisest thing we could ever have is a healthy dose of the fear of the Lord. The evidence that we understand what it means is when we depart from evil ways.

CONFESSION: I have a healthy respect for the fear of the Lord!

PRAYER

Father, I honor You, I lift up Your holy name, Jesus. I will honor my mother and father by respecting them. I will have a healthy fear of the Lord in my heart so that I will respectfully walk according to Your Word. You are my refuge, my shelter, and my confidence during the storms of life. In Jesus' name, amen.

Day 20: Very Funny, God!

Then Abraham fell upon his face, and laughed, and said in his heart, Shall a child be born unto him that is an hundred years old? and shall Sarah, that is ninety years old, bear? (Genesis 17:17 KJV)

Have you ever shared a dream or vision that you feel God has called you to do, and when you share it with someone, they laugh at you? Why would someone do that? Because they believe that you can't accomplish such a thing. It can be quite disheartening for sure. But they should laugh at the vision than at you. Davids brother's laughed and ridiculed him—or should I say, they tried to belittle him by telling him to go back and watch the few sheep he was caring for. I challenge you, Champion: Be like David and ignore them. You need to be concerned and careful that you do not laugh at what God has called you to do.

Sarai also laughed when the Lord told her that she was going to have a child. Let's read:

So she laughed silently to herself and said, "How could a worn-out woman like me enjoy such pleasure, especially when my master—my husband—is also so old?" Then the Lord said to Abraham, "Why did Sarah laugh? Why did she say, 'Can an old woman like me have a baby?' **Is anything too hard for the Lord?** I will return about this time next year, and Sarah will have a son." (Genesis 18:12-14 NLT)

Is anything too hard for the Lord? Is what God called you to do too hard for Him to do through you? Now there is a question only you can answer. Don't try to argue with God—you will not win. Sarah tried to argue, and I think it is quite humorous: "Sarah was afraid, so she denied it, saying, 'I didn't laugh.' But the Lord said, 'No, you did laugh'" (Genesis 18:15 NLT)

No, you did laugh; end of argument!

Have you ever doubted what God has called you to do? Have you said, "Lord, that dream is too big for me. Can you give me a smaller one?" Maybe your thinking, *Lord, I'm way too young or old, and I don't have the proper training or education to do what I sense you're calling me to do. And I don't have access to that kind of money. Very funny, God, it's simply impossible!* And you laugh at the absurdity of it.

It may seem impossible for you to complete the massive task that you sense in your heart of hearts, but keep this in mind—God designed it that way. He wants you to trust Him every step of the way!

ATTITUDE CHECK: If you desire to do something *for* God, you will miss the mark. But if you have a desire to do something *with* God, you are on the right path.

CONFESSION: I can do all things through Christ Jesus, who empowers me!

PRAYER

Father God, I repent for making You too small in my eyes. I know that nothing is too hard for You. As Isaiah the prophet declared, "Here I am, Lord, send me." I want to do greater things WITH You, not FOR You. I will learn to live and walk by faith as You lead me. Help me share my vision, plan, and dreams to those I love and respect in the Lord to keep myself accountable. I realize now, Lord, the plans You give me will always be bigger than me and impossible to accomplish without Your help. All things are possible with You. Amen.

Day 21: Your Plan B Is Not Better than God's Plan A

And Abraham said unto God, O that Ishmael might live before thee! (Genesis 17:18 KJV)

In the effort to fulfill your God-dream or vision for your life, there will always be times when you will hit an impasse. Impasses are not all bad. They can actually be good because it can be a great time to test and try your faith. I like to say that God works in the delay. When we pray without seeing the results of what we are hoping for, it is a real character builder. An *impasse* is a delay, a situation in which no progress seems possible, **primarily because of disagreement.**

You may be at an impasse right now that has caused you to come to a standstill. There seems to be no progress, and it appears to be humanly impossible for this to come to pass. This is a crucial place to be in.

I want to point out that I highlighted **"especially because of disagreement,"** because when you don't know what to do next, you have to be very careful not to say something or do something stupid. The worst thing you can do at an impasse is try to figure out a "plan B."

When you are in an impasse, be careful not to reason within yourself and disagree with what God has called you to do. At this stage, many people begin to redesign God's plan, and that is dangerous territory.

Look what Abram said when he came to an impasse in his God plan. "O that Ishmael might live before thee!" Ishmael may have been his first son, but it was from a sexual relationship with Sarai's slave girl, Hagar.

When God told Abram that he was going to be a father of nations, God didn't intend for him to figure it out on his own and have sex with a slave girl to give birth to "Plan B." If you read his story carefully, it never said that Abram consulted God about going to Hagar. When Sarai suggested that Abram have sex with Hagar, he might have run to her tent to fulfill the promise his way. We *must hear from God* before we take any step, especially when we have a plan B

Here's some food for thought: Out of Ishmael was birthed the Arab nations. Abraham was the first Hebrew or Jew. As you can see today, many Arab counties despise the nation of Israel, even today. That, my friend, is the long-term consequence of not sticking to Plan A. Plan B misses the mark. Having children with women besides your wife is not Plan A. It's Plan B, which can cause you many worries and problems. (Please note that this doesn't mean any children born out of wedlock are bad people. It just causes situations and scenarios that can be uncomfortable for everyone.)

My advice to you: stick to the plan (Plan A, that is.)

CONFESSION: God has a plan for my life!

PRAYER

Father God, I desire to do Your will in my life. I want to stay the course; I don't want to drift or sway from the plan You gave me. I desire Your wisdom, Your input, and the leading of Your Holy Spirit to keep me on course. When I come to an impasse, I will not allow it to become a mountain that I cannot pass. I will speak to it; I will stand firm to your plan because I can do all things

SOAR IN HIS STRENGTH

through You, Jesus. You will empower me to do what You called me to do. I do not have to fear, doubt, or question You. Plan A is what I am called to fulfill, and I will accomplish plan A in my life. I look forward to my reward of You saying to me: Well done, good and faithful servant. Amen.

Day 22: What to Do When You Lose Jesus

Now this is what the Lord says to the family of Israel:
"Come back to me and live! (Amos 5:4 NLT)

We all lose our way once in a while. But keep in mind that no one crashes in burns in one day. For example, when a godly man or woman loses their way and sins and it is made public, many folks will say, "I'm so surprised, it just doesn't make sense," or "how could this happen to them?" I want to assure you that it started way before it happened. It was what I call a "slow fade."

These godly people faded away from their devotions or started looking at porn, or maybe they lost control of their drinking or pain medication. Maybe their loving marriage was beginning to dissolve. Then "POW" it happened, and everyone is shocked—everyone but God. He saw them start to drift from Him weeks or months before they fell into sin. By the time they drifted so far, it may have seemed to them that Jesus had left them.

Listen, if you've drifted away from the Lord, you're not the only one who left Jesus behind:

> After the celebration was over, they started home to Nazareth, but Jesus stayed behind in Jerusalem. His parents didn't miss him at first, because they assumed he was among the other travelers. But when he didn't show up that evening, they started looking for him among their relatives and friends. When they couldn't

find him, they went back to Jerusalem to search for him there. (Luke 2:43-45 NLT)

Mary must have been shocked, and Joseph stunned when they realized that they lost the Son of God. They lost the Savior of the world—and they must have been in panic mode!

One year our family went to a famous theme park on vacation. One day on the trip started as a sunny day, but then it began to sprinkle for an hour or so. My oldest granddaughter had a yellow raincoat on that we had purchased at the park. Then it happened: she was by my side, and in a moment she disappeared. I cried out, "where's Ari?" As I was beginning to panic, I turned to look at the crowd and saw hundreds of children who were all wearing yellow raincoats. My terror went to a new level until I heard my daughter say, "Dad, she's right here." Wow, was I relieved! A little embarrassed but more relieved.

Mary and Joseph lost Jesus, the Son of God, and they didn't find him for three whole days! They did something that we should all do when we feel that we have left Jesus behind in our life. "And when they found him not, **they turned back again to Jerusalem**, seeking him" (Luke 2:45 KJV).

Have you lost Jesus in your life? Have you left Him behind? Then do what Mary and Joseph did and turn and go back to Jerusalem. Go back to the Bible, go back to prayer, go back to church, go to your prayer closet. Then you will find Him.

CONFESSION: Today I come back to You, Lord!

PRAYER

Lord, I'm so sorry for drifting from you again. You have been so good to me. Your Word says that I can come boldly into your throne room of grace to obtain mercy and grace in time of need. Lord, I need Your grace, Your mercy, and Your presence. I know You already have forgiven me; I have that blessed assurance deep in my heart of hearts. Thank You, Lord, I ask for Your Holy Spirit to refresh my walk so I can walk in the Spirit again and not fulfill the lust of the flesh. Amen.

Day 23: GOD IS A REWARDER, NOT A WITHHOLDER

But without faith it is impossible to please him: for he that cometh to God must believe that he is, and that he is a rewarder of them that diligently seek him. (Hebrews 11:6 KJV)

If anyone has gotten a bad rap, it's the Almighty God, and it continues today. My mom used to say, "God is going to punish you for doing that." To a child, that can be frightening. But where did my mom come up with that? How did she equate God with someone who is out to get someone for every little bad thing they do? I can sum it up in one word: *religion*.

This mentality isn't just found in the religious sector but crossed over into the secular business world. For example, insurance companies label certain situations an "act of God." They often consider a flood, earthquake, or storm to be considered an act of God. Do you see that? If something cannot be explained, they want to say it's God's fault.

I remember reading the above text early on in my walk with God, and when it opened my eyes, the walls of doubt began to fall, and a rush of possibilities flooded my spirit; God is a *rewarder*, not a withholder. The "Que sera sera" mentality was torn down. I knew that God existed, of course, but now I was ready to deal some major damage to the kingdom of darkness.

I was wise enough to know that money or possessions won't just fall out of heaven, but I also knew that John the Baptist said, " A man can receive nothing, except it be given him from heaven" (John 3:27 KJV).

Here are a few other things you may not realize:

- Did you know you have not because you asked not? (See James 4:2.)

- Did you know your motive for asking is important? (See James 4:3.)

- Do you believe God will do what you ask for? (See Mark 11:24.)

- Did you know that if you delight yourself in the Lord, He will give you the desires of your heart? (See Ps. 37:4)

I'm sure you have heard that God is not a respecter of persons. But allow me to challenge your comfort zone: Even though God is not a respecter of persons, He is a respecter of one's faith. Faith moves God. The scripture above says that He (God) is a *rewarder* of those who diligently seek Him. Here, the keyword is *diligently*, which means to be steady, earnest, or an energetic effort. After all, it doesn't say He rewards those who "casually seek Him," or "when the spirit moves them," or "when one has time to seek Him." No, it says He is a *rewarder* of those who diligently seek him. The word seek refers to worship—giving full attention to God. You can do that by praying, singing to Him at church or home, praying in the spirit, studying the Word, etc.

In closing, I would like to share a story in the Bible about an old widow who wanted justice and never gave up. Let's read:

And he spake a parable unto them to this end, that men ought always to pray, and not to faint; saying, There was in a city a judge, which feared not God, neither regarded man: And there was a widow in that city; and she came unto him, saying, Avenge me of mine adversary. And he would not for a while: but afterward he said within himself, Though I fear not God, nor regard man; Yet because this widow troubleth me, I will avenge her, lest by her continual coming she weary me. And the Lord said, Hear what the unjust judge saith. And shall not God avenge his own elect, which cry day and night unto him, though he bear long with them? I tell you that he will avenge them speedily. Nevertheless when the Son of man cometh, shall he find faith on the earth?" (Luke 18:1-8 KJV)

Through this parable, Jesus was wondering if He would find faith on the earth among His believers when he returns. I want to answer yes to Jesus' question, and I am sure you do too!

CONFESSION: God is a rewarder, not a withholder!

PRAYER

Father God, Thank You for the promises in Your Word. I repent of my spiritual slothfulness. Help me be diligent in prayer and in advancing the kingdom of God. In Jesus' name, amen.

Day 24: Are You Running in the Opposite Direction of Your Dream?

> The Lord gave this message to Jonah son of Amittai: "Get up and go to the great city of Nineveh"...But Jonah got up and went in the opposite direction to get away from the Lord. (Jonah 1:1-3 NLT)

I can point out three things right away from the passage above:

- First Point: Do what God says; it's called obedience.
- Second Point: This wasn't Jonah's dream.
- Third Point: Resistance is futile.

Jonah resisted doing what God told him to do. I'll save you some time and heartache: don't do that to God. You see, Jonah fought the Lord, and the Lord won. God always gets his man/woman, even if he makes a whale swallow you and transport you to the place you resisted going.

Like us, Jonah had issues. If he had only trusted God, things would have gone so much easier for him! The book of Jonah doesn't share anything about what Jonah's life dream was. But it does share the importance of living a life of obedience.

Without hope, life can be miserable. Without a vision, a dream, or purpose, people will perish.

> Where there is no vision, the people perish: but he that keepeth the law, happy is he. (Proverbs 29:18 KJV)

Here is the point I am going for today: To live out the dream God gave you, there will always something you have to do first that your flesh *does not* want to do.

It's not about condemnation; instead, this is about having confidence in God. God will test you. The devil will tempt you. God gives us the power to overcome temptation and pass every test that comes our way.

God has a plan and purpose in your life, and today is another day to prepare for it. God is always preparing us for the future. The Holy Spirit may have been speaking to you about a bad attitude you've been carrying toward something or someone. He wants you to drop it. Maybe there's been a sinful behavior you are ignoring. God is saying, "Talk to Me about it," so don't ignore His voice. God wants to take you someplace, He wants to lead you into your dream or vision, but first, the attitude or sinful behaviors must go.

> Therefore, since we are surrounded by such a huge crowd of witnesses to the life of faith, let us strip off every weight that slows us down, especially the sin that so easily trips up. And let us run with endurance the race God has set before us. We do this by keeping our eyes on Jesus, the champion who initiates and perfects our faith. Because of the joy awaiting him, he endured the cross, disregarding its shame. Now he is seated in the place of honor beside God's throne. (Hebrews 12:1-2 NLT)

Don't be swallowed up by the ways of the world. Just do what the Holy Spirit directs you to do.

DECLARATION: Resisting God is futile.

PRAYER

Jesus, You are my High Priest. You understand everything I'm going through. You have compassion on me because You were tempted just like I was, but You submitted to the Father and resisted the enemy. Teach me, Holy Spirit, to do the same. In Jesus' name, amen.

Day 25: Blessed Are the Peacemakers, Not Peacekeepers

Blessed are the peacemakers; for they shall be called the children of God. (Matthew 5:9 KJV)

I admire the men and women throughout my life who would pull me aside (except, of course, my wife—just kidding!) and point something out to me that I said or did that hurt them or others. Of course, it matters how they do it; if done with pure motives and using the right words and tone of voice, it has made a great difference in my life.

I appreciated the times when what they had to say helped me improve an area of my life or showed me how I should make the needed change. These are great examples of godly men and women, for sure.

For someone to confront you regarding your behavior takes an ingredient that many believers seem to lack. That ingredient is courage. Courage is a core element that is evident in the real peacemakers of God. But there is a stark difference between someone who is a godly peacemaker and merely a peacekeeper.

A peacekeeper won't want to rock the boat in people's lives. Maybe they either hope the issue goes away by itself or that someone else will address it. Maybe they believe in magic. Unfortunately, there's no such thing as magic, especially when it comes to building healthy relationships. Relationships need to be cultivated. Sometimes things need to be planted, or uprooted, built up, or torn down. When a peacekeeper consistently ignores these offenses, there can be serious repercussions.

For example: if the issue is allowed to continue and is not dealt with, over time, offense after offense can build up, and then at any given moment, there can be an explosive argument. This can happen due to a lack of communication or procrastinating or refusing to confront a matter.

Let's look at the courageous advice Jesus gives us:

> Moreover if thy brother shall trespass against thee, **go and tell him his fault** between thee and him **alone**: if he shall hear thee, thou hast **gained** thy brother. (Matthew 18:15 KJV)

Jesus instructs us:

- **To go to him:** It takes courage and obedience.
- **Tell him his fault**: Communicating everything
- **Hast gained thy brother:** Your relationship has been not just saved, but strengthened

It's your choice; you can choose not to rock the boat, peacekeeper—or you can choose to be God's peacemaker and strengthen relationships. It takes wisdom and courage.

DECLARATION: I am a peacemaker for God!

PRAYER

Lord, I know You have created us to have relationships with You and with others. I ask You for the wisdom, courage, and discernment necessary for me to be a cultivator of godly relationships. Father, help me to recognize the peacemakers that You send my way to confront me of fleshly behavior. In fact, Lord, I invite them into my life for my benefit. Amen!

Day 26: Facing Off with Temptation

> If you think you are standing strong, be careful not to fall.
> The temptations in your life are no different from what
> others experience. And God is faithful. He will not allow
> the temptation to be more than you can stand. When you
> are tempted, he will show you a way out so that you can
> endure. (1 Corinthians 10:12-13 NLT)

I'm sure you have seen fight night promotional pictures of two fighters facing each other off, glaring into each other's eyes. This is a good picture of how we face-off with our temptations. But the good news is that it's not us doing the face-off; instead, Jesus is facing off for us.

> He that committeth sin is of the devil; for the devil
> sinneth from the beginning. For this purpose the Son of
> God was manifested, that he might destroy the works of
> the devil. (1 John 3:8 KJV)

By faith, we know that Jesus destroyed the works of the devil. So, spiritually speaking, it's not a face-off at all, but a wipe-out!

> Submit yourselves therefore to God. Resist the devil, and
> he will flee from you. (James 4:7 KJV)

Temptation is no match for the child of God who submits to God. When we submit to God, there is a transfer of the GodStrength we need in times of trouble—and that includes times of temptation.

When you have been tempted, some demonic creature didn't approach you, wearing a red suit with a pointed tail and two horns protruding out of their forehead, holding a pitchfork. Actually, that would be much better. At least you would recognize that you are being tempted.

Unfortunately, temptations **do not** come that way, but they come in attractive packages from "the beautiful side of evil."

> And no marvel; for Satan himself is transformed into an angel of light. (2 Corinthians 11:14 KJV)

Your temptation will most likely engulf you with something you desire very much, something you feel you have been deprived of and you deserve or have a right to. That's very dangerous ground to stand on. Take heed lest you fall!

There are many things to talk about concerning temptation that we will talk about another day, but I will leave you with a tip for the day concerning the temptations you are facing at the moment.

When temptation comes, simply but powerfully, submit to God and PRAISE HIM!

> My brethren, count it all joy when ye fall into divers temptations; Knowing this, that the trying of your faith worketh patience. But let patience have her perfect work, that ye may be perfect and entire, wanting nothing. (James 1:2-4 KJV)

DECLARATION: I will praise the Lord in the face of temptation!

PRAYER

Father, I thank and praise You for all You did for me on the cross. But, Lord, You didn't stop there; you poured Your Spirit out on Pentecost and transferred Your GodStrength to mankind. I submit to You in praise today when I am being tempted, and I will rejoice as the devil flees from me. In Jesus' name, amen.

Day 27: Your Faith Must and Will Be Tested

For you know that when your faith is tested, your endurance has a chance to grow. (James 1:3 NLT)

Whether it's a testing, a temptation, or a severe tribulation, they are all necessary for our lives if we wish to grow strong in the Lord and in the power of His might.

I would definitely not want to be on a plane flying 30,000 feet in the air when the captain comes on the speaker and says, "Welcome aboard flight #221. This flight, my friends, is this airplane's maiden voyage."

My eyebrows would raise, and I would scan the plane for others who may be thinking like me at the moment. And what was I thinking? "Oh my goodness!" I've flown enough in my life to know that we will hit turbulence at least once, if not several times. I want to make sure that this plane passed all tests and inspections before I got in it.

The good news is that planes go through many exhausting tests and examinations before it even takes its maiden flight. The wings are bend to almost 90 degrees to see what the breaking point is, and they make sure they surpass it. They even throw dead birds through a powerful air pressure gun at the cockpit to test the windshield and into the engines to make sure they won't cut out during flight if they encounter a flock of birds. This happened on January 15, 2009, when a US Airways Airbus A320 encountered a flock of geese and both engines were disabled. The good news is that the captain was a proven and tested man and landed the plane on the Hudson River. All 155 passengers and crew members landed and evacuated safely. For the whole story, do an Internet search on Captain Sully.

We can and must be trained and tested like Captain Sully, so to speak. God is preparing you *now* for your next encounter.

God wants you to pass every test. He is not trying to trip you up or shove you in the chest to start a fight. Instead, He's getting you ready for Goliath—that mountain you're facing or that moment when someone needs you to be strong inside. That's what it's all about—the inward strength to overcome. When the Father looks at us, He only wants to see His Son in us.

Here is God's goal for your life:

> For whom he did foreknow, he also did predestinate **to be conformed to the image of his Son**, that he might be the firstborn among many brethren. (Romans 8:29 KJV)

Temptations are used by God to strengthen our endurance so we can finish the race. But *we must* recognize *the source* of our strength.

Now for my last illustration concerning our faith being tested:

Trees need wind to blow against them because it causes their root system to grow deeper and that helps support the tree as it grows taller. So as the tree accepts the strong wind as a blessing that helps it grow we also should rejoice for the testing winds of faith that blow against us.

CONFESSION: With You, Lord, I am stronger than ever!

PRAYER

Father, there are times that it seems like I go from one attack to another. Let me see from Your perspective. I must see this situation with the eyes of faith. I should be afraid in the natural, but through You, I am strong, I can endure longer, and do to greater things than I could ever imagine. In Jesus' name, amen.

Day 28: A Great Reminder

You must influence them; do not let them influence you!
(Jeremiah 15:19 NLT)

In the verse above, the Lord was speaking to Jeremiah while he was in a weakened state in his ministry. The prophet was questioning things that were happening around him, and God was gracious to give him a direct answer. He told him: You must influence them; do not let them influence you.

This is great advice for us today. Maybe you woke up feeling discouraged or just weak in your faith, but my prayer is that this will be a reminder for you today to let your light shine in your work area, neighborhood, or university. Leadership is influence. Good influence is good leadership; bad influence is bad leadership.

The world can be very attractive at times and very tempting. There are times when we see our worldly coworkers, schoolmates, and even our friends say or do something "worldly" that we remember. We may even be tempted to repeat what they say or do when we have a frustrating moment. But remember, we are to influence them, not allow them to influence us.

One of the greatest reminders in my discipleship upbringing is the passage found in the book of Romans;

> Don't copy the behavior and customs of this world, but let God transform you into a new person by changing the way you think. Then you will learn to know God's will for you, which is good and pleasing and perfect. (Romans 12:2 NLT)

The NIV says, "Do not conform to the pattern of this world."

Chaplain Ronnie Melancon made a statement that is so true, "Show me your friends, and I will show you your future." The Bible says: "As iron sharpens iron, so one person sharpens another" (Proverbs 27:17 NIV). Watch who you hang out with; you will pick up their habits, words, and actions.

If you do not have friends, my heart goes out to you, but let me be straight with you. You have a friend in Jesus. I suggest that you stay close to Him and go where His family (His church) hangs out.

In closing, consider this:

> We are therefore Christ's ambassadors, as though God were making his appeal through us. We implore you on Christ's behalf: Be reconciled to God. (2 Corinthians 5:20 NIV)

Do you see that? We are ambassadors—senior representatives—from the kingdom of heaven.

So can you really afford a BAD DAY? Of course not, but if you do, make the necessary adjustments and apologies, and get back up. We have to remain strong in the Lord and in the power of His might so our lives will cause those who surround us to hunger and thirst for the things of God.

CONFESSION: I am an ambassador of Christ!

PRAYER

Father, You know what I am going through, and it seems that sometimes I am going to break. If it were not for You and the call on my life, I would give it up. I am a child of God, and Your hand is upon me for sure. I will let my light shine today. May my life be filled with Your salt to make people thirsty for the life that I have, not the other way around. Thank You, Jesus, amen.

Day 29: The Call of God and Responding to His Call

As Jesus was walking along, he saw a man named Matthew sitting at his tax collector's booth. "Follow me and be my disciple," Jesus said to him. So Matthew got up and followed him. (Matthew 9:9 NLT)

When I read this passage, it reminds me of those of us who heard the call of God and the courage it took to respond to it and follow Jesus. Matthew didn't qualify to be a disciple, yet Jesus called him anyway, just like you. Jesus simply chose him as He chose you.

This one sentence spoken by Jesus resonated in Matthew's heart of hearts. He recognized it to be a true and honorable thing to do. Then he immediately got off his seat, left his profession, and fully followed Jesus. His enthusiasm didn't end there, but he paid the price to become a disciple of Jesus Christ. How do I know that? Because he penned the book of Matthew. He was tired of the life he was living, a life with no honor or dignity among his people. Tax collectors were known as shysters and swindlers, and the worst part was that he was a Jew who was swindling his own people.

Some of you reading this may have had to leave a job due to conscience's sake like Matthew did. It is a difficult thing to do but necessary, to say the least. When I first got saved, I was working in a nightclub as a disc-jockey. The atmosphere was vexing my righteous soul, similar to what happened to Abraham's nephew Lot when he lived in Sodom. I loved my job, but I knew I had to get out of it. There was no way I was going to grow in the Lord if I remained in that environment.

Six months after I got saved, I got up and followed Jesus. I stopped and hugged my boss, Mr. Mike, and wept. Why? I loved him and I loved what

I was doing. At the time, I assumed many people would follow me, but not one person did. They must have loved the environment.

So where were you when God called you out of darkness and into His marvelous light? Hopefully, you didn't have to leave your job or occupation. Many of us did not have to, but you got up and followed Jesus and became salt and light in your workplace. I have heard believers say, "It seems like I work in hell, and I cannot wait to get out of there!" Really? Don't you think God was wise enough to strategically place you in that position so the light of the gospel could shine through you? We have to believe it.

I have worked in places where even the boss looked me in the eye and said, "You know, Christians don't make it here." Well, I did, and when I left that job in good standing for another, I looked him in the eye and said, "I won, you know." He said, What are you talking about?" I said, "You know, I won." He responded with a smile on his face and said, "Yes, you did." I had a Christian friend who stayed at that job, and when the boss was diagnosed with a brain tumor, my friend led him to the Lord. Remember, you never know who is watching you!

CONFESSION: I will follow You today, Jesus!

PRAYER

Lord, You know what I'm facing at the moment. You have the strategy to help me deal with it. No matter how long this goes on, through You, I am an overcomer, a child of God. I will keep both hands on the plow and fix my eyes on You, Jesus, for You are my Champion. You said that we would have tribulations in the world, and it has been very true, but You have helped me overcome every one of them, and You will help me with the one I am facing now. In Jesus' name, amen.

Day 30: Do You Want Your Life Changed?

Come close to Go, and God will come close to you. (James 4:8 NLT)

Draw nigh to God, and he will draw nigh to you. (James 4:8 KJV)

You have just read a spiritual law that no one can ever change. Drawing near to God every day will change your life dramatically. Your devotions are that important. I went twenty-six years without a personal relationship with Jesus, so for twenty-six years, I really didn't pray. Oh, I had religious conversations with somebody in the spiritual realm, but not face to face with the one I love now.

This is not just a spiritual law; this passage is a promise from your Lord and Savior Jesus that if you will pull yourself out of your busy—and sometimes chaotic—world and go to your prayer closet, you will find out that He is already there waiting for you. Just draw near.

It can be a moment at a red light or some quality time in your living room or wherever your prayer closet may be. Just get there and make it a habit to do so.

Let look into a word that Jesus uses regarding prayer.

But thou, when thou prayest, enter into thy closet, and when thou hast shut thy door, pray to thy Father which is in secret; and thy Father which seeth in secret shall reward thee openly. (Matthew 6:6 KJV)

The word *closet* is an interesting word in the Greek. It means "a dispensary or magazine." A *dispensary* is a place where things are dispersed. The Holy Spirit disperses what you need in the spirit. A magazine is where supplies are handed out, and in military terms, a magazine is a place where ammunition is kept. Wow! Say this: My God will supply all of my needs according to His riches in heaven!

Why wouldn't you draw near to God when you know all of this? Maybe because the enemy has lied to you, saying that you aren't worthy or you don't have the faith to receive. Or worst yet: "What's the use?"

Maybe you are saying, "I'm too busy to pray." Can you hear yourself saying that? It doesn't sound right, does it? My suggestion is: stop listening to yourself and follow the sweet tender voice of the Lord, saying, "Come away with Me."

What happens when you begin to draw near to God every day? So many things will happen that I can't list them all, but here are a few:

- You will begin to see your prayers answered more frequently.
- You will sharpen your spiritual hearing. This is important because prayer isn't all about us talking to God but listening to God's Spirit. He communicates with us by His Spirit, not our natural mind. Listening will help you to become Christlike. He will speak to you about your behavior, how you have been treating your spouse, your friends, etc.
- Spending time with Jesus every day will show in your countenance. Do you remember reading about how Moses' face was shining because he was speaking to the Lord in Exodus 34:29? Your countenance also will shine.
- Your attitude will be brighter, and the burden you are caring will seem lighter.

QUESTION: Why are you still here? Run to God with all of your heart!

CONFESSION: Jesus, I am coming to You!

PRAYER

Lord, I want to stop lying to myself by making excuses for why I don't pray. Help me, Holy Spirit, to spend quality time with You; I want to spend time with You, not for my sake, but for the sake of those in my life. In Jesus' name, amen.

Day 31: What Does the Mississippi River Have to Do with Following Jesus?

For as many as are led by the Spirit of God, they are the sons of God. (Romans 8:14 KJV)

Today is another day and another opportunity for you to walk in the Spirit. Aren't you excited? You should be because the Holy Spirit puts all the fun in Christianity, especially in this day and age!

When you learn to follow Him at times, your spirit will leap for joy when He always seems to pull through for you.

There are times when I wonder why things haven't gone my way or why something has not come to pass as I expected. Our human nature tends to play the "blame game" with God and others. We have to learn to take full responsibility for following the Lord and His precious Holy Spirit.

God is smarter than you. But according to 1 Corinthians 2:16, you have the mind of Christ when you walk in the Spirit.

When our human mind is connected with the Holy Spirit and we are lined up with the Word of God, then we have the mind of Christ to help us figure things out. There are many things that can disrupt this anointed connection; two of them are ignorance and pride.

Being *ignorant* means that you simply do not know something. Daniel 11:32 (KJV) says: "But the people that do know their God shall be strong, and do exploits." You will never do great exploits if you do not know your God.

Look at what the Bible says about pride:

Yea, all of you be subject one to another, and be clothed with humility: for God resisteth the proud, and giveth grace to the humble. (1 Peter 5:5 KJV)

Humility is God's antidote for our pride. God will resist us if we are not humble.

I have had the opportunities to fly across our great country and beyond to minister the gospel. One sunny clear day, the plane I was in flew over the mighty Mississippi River. It was beautiful, to say the least. As I was google-eyed on the river, I noticed that it doesn't look like it's appearance on the map. On the map, this river seemed to run almost in a straight line, but from the air, the river was looping in and out and back and forth over again. It almost made a complete loop with an island in the middle too. Needless to say, I was fascinated by it.

It prompted me to ask the Lord this question: "Lord, why do rivers seem to loop like that endlessly at times?" His response was quite astonishing. God replied, "Rivers are like my Spirit and will always flow where it finds the least resistance."

Look back at our starting verse again: "For as many as are led by the Spirit are the sons of God." Surrender your life to Him today, and then you will discover where He is leading you.

CONFESSION: Good morning, Holy Spirit!

PRAYER

Father, I surrender all to You, my precious Lord. I do not want to resist Your Holy Spirit today. I want to follow Him in whatever He has for me to say or do today. With Him living inside of me, I can be who I am called to be, and I can do all things through Him. In Jesus' name, amen.

95

Day 32: Are You a Faithful Person?

His lord said unto him, Well done, thou good and faithful servant. (Matthew 25:21 KJV)

F*aithful* is used to describe someone who can be relied upon and is worthy of trust, who shows themselves faithful.[4]

Faithfulness is a fruit of the Spirit, which means that if you are a believer, faithfulness infused into your born-again spirit, and all you have to do is yield to what God put in you. But this faithfulness is not *your* faithfulness; it is Jesus' faithfulness in you.

When you were born again, God didn't empower *your* character, He empowered you with *His* character. That, my friend, is a whole new ball game.

So your prayer should not be, "Lord, give me some faithfulness," but, "Lord, help me yield to Your faithfulness in me."

God is faithful, and He will be faithful to you. You can be unfaithful, but He will be faithful to you if you come boldly into His throne of grace to ask for mercy and grace in time of need (Hebrews 4:16).

Don't look for a pat on the back today from anyone but from God.

> And whatsoever ye do, do it heartily, as to the Lord, and not unto men; Knowing that of the Lord ye shall receive the reward of the inheritance: for ye serve the Lord Christ. (Colossians 3:23-24 KJV)

4. "G4103 - pistos - Strong's Greek Lexicon (KJV)." Blue Letter Bible. Accessed 3 May, 2021. https://www.blueletterbible.org//lang/lexicon/lexicon.cfm?Strongs=G4103&t=KJV.

This isn't easy; if it was, even sinners would be able to do it. Know that God sees what you are doing, and promotion comes from God, not man. Remain faithful; it will pay off!

One day at work, the foreman had to find someone to do something over again because of a mistake someone made. He said out loud, "Oh man, now I have to take one of my best men of the line to do this." Then he called my name. I joyfully did the rework; I felt so honored.

Are you one of the best workers at your job? You should be. Do you show up for work early? Do you cheat on your time sheet? You shouldn't.

Another day in the factory I was doing a spot welding job, and at the end of the day my group leader told me to put down that I did seventy pieces per hour. I told him that I couldn't do that because I only did sixty-one pieces per hour. He responded, "Everyone does it, don't worry. Just put it down." I responded, "Just because everyone does it, doesn't make it right. I am not going to lie."

He got upset with me and walked away, smoking his pipe. Then suddenly he turned to me and said, "You know, Danny, there has to be some hypocrite in you, and I'm going to find it."

Have you been faithful to your spouse? Your children? Faithfulness holds a lot of weight when it comes to God and His kingdom. Take a look at the rest of our starting verse for today:

> His lord said unto him, Well done, thou good and faithful servant: thou hast been faithful over a few things, I will make thee ruler over many things: enter thou into the joy of thy lord. (Matthew 25:21 KJV)

If you are a believer, then you are filled with His Spirit and His faithfulness is in you. Confess the following today:

CONFESSION: Lord, I will be faithful today.

PRAYER

Thank You, Jesus, for being faithful to me. I want You to live Your life through me. After all, it's all about Your life through me. Lord, thank You for the BEST LIFE EVER!

Day 33: What Does God and Michelangelo Have in Common?

I will praise thee; for I am fearfully and wonderfully made: marvellous are thy works; and that my soul knoweth right well. (Psalms 139:14 KJV)

You may have already heard this, but Michelangelo was asked once, "How do you make your masterpieces?" His response was, "The sculpture is already complete within the marble block before I start my work. It is already there; I just have to chisel away the superfluous material."

As an artist, Michelangelo had an amazing ability to see what he wanted to make before he took a hammer and chisel to the marble block.

It's the same with God, but to a greater level, of course. Look at this powerful message from the Bible:

Blessed be the God and Father of our Lord Jesus Christ, who hath blessed us with all spiritual blessings in heavenly places in Christ: **According as he hath chosen us in him before the foundation of the world,** that we should be holy and without blame before him in love: Having predestinated us unto the adoption of children by Jesus Christ to himself, according to the good pleasure of his will. (Ephesians 1:3-5 KJV)

He chose you before the foundations of the world were laid. In the Apostle Paul's sermon to the Greeks on Mars Hill, he said that God also chose our birth date and where we would live. Look at this passage:

SOAR IN HIS STRENGTH

> From one man he made all the nations, that they should inhabit the whole earth; and he marked out their appointed times in history and the boundaries of their lands. (Acts 17:26 NIV)

See that? God has a plan for you. In the next verse, He enlighten us as to why He placed us exactly where He put us on planet Earth: to worship Him.

> God did this so that they would seek him and perhaps reach out for him and find him, though he is not far from any one of us. "For in him we live and move and have our being." (Acts 17:27-28 NIV)

As you seek the Lord, He will lead you, guide you, instruct you, and correct you. When you go through trials and tribulations, He will also remind you who are in Him or He may even chastise you when necessary. Don't let the word *chastise* scare you, it simply means He will train you, but sometimes the training is difficult. If you don't listen to His soft voice, it can open yourself up to His judgment. So if you do not repent or change your behavior, He may expose your wrongdoing to loved ones or to the general public. Never forget that He is the potter, and we are the clay. We are the ones who are supposed to conform to God—not God to us.

> Does not the potter have the right to make out of the same lump of clay some pottery for special purposes and some for common use? (Romans 9:21 NIV)

Here's another story about Michelangeo that I've adapted to today's culture, and even if it's not true, it still teaches a spiritual principle. One day while Michelangelo was working for a long time on the Sistine Chapel, one of his friends came in and yelled out to him in strong Italian accent, "Hey, Michael, what are you doing? Come on down, we're having a pizza pie. Hurry up, Michael!" Michelangelo responded, "You'll have to wait, my paisan, I have to make sure this is done right."

He friend responded, "Come on Michael, the pizza pie is gonna get cold. Nobody will notice it up there anyway," Michelangelo responded with a resounding, "God will see it."

God sees you! He sees what He made you to be even if you are not walking in your calling and destiny yet.

CONFESSION: God, You are the Potter, I am the clay!

PRAYER

Lord, I surrender the very core of who I am to You. In Jesus' name, amen.

Day 34: Think about This the Next Time You Reach into Your Cupboard

But in a great house there are not only vessels of gold and of silver, but also of wood and of earth; and some to honour, and some to dishonour. (2 Timothy 2:20 KJV)

When it comes to cups, glasses, or mugs, I am very peculiar. You know what? So is God.

I will not drink cold milk in any plastic container. It has to be a made of clear, see-through glass. It tastes so good (especially with some cookies!). I also have certain cups I use when drinking coffee and tea. I don't fancy a big mug, but rather a restaurant-like cup. But when it comes to hot chocolate, it's has to be in a mug (along with marshmallow topping). So good!

This is exactly what the Lord does when He needs a job done. First of all, none of us qualify, except by His grace. But he is looking for those who have a heart for Him. So He goes throughout the kingdom's "cupboards," looking for that certain vessel to us, and when He finds them, He reaches and chooses them to be a vessel of honor.

There is much to do to be a vessel of honor. Read the very next verse:

If a man therefore purge himself from these, he shall be a vessel unto honour, sanctified, and meet for the master's use, and prepared unto every good work. (2 Timothy 2:21 KJV)

Did you see that? If someone purges themselves, they will become a vessel of honor. So it's a choice to walk in His grace.

I tell everyone, especially the young men, who come into my office to be mentored, "When you sin (and you will sin), clean your cup as soon as possible." Then I reach for my coffee cup on my desk (which is perfectly shaped and meets all of my needs) and show them the inside of it. I ask them, "Would you drink from this cup?" They would say no. when I ask them why not, they typically respond, "Because it's dirty." Then when I ask if they would drink from it if I cleaned it, they say yes.

My point is that you should never eliminate yourself from kingdom purpose. When you sin, confess or acknowledge your sin immediately. Don't wait for a feeling. Don't wait until you feel guilty. The Holy Spirit was grieved the very moment you sinned, so please know that your sin was already forgiven two thousand years ago. Just begin to thank the Lord for His forgiveness.

When you begin to acknowledge your sin to the Lord, the devil and his demons will begin to scream at you, "You're not worthy to be saved. How could you do that? You knew better. You've been walking with God for a long time, and God will never forgive your for that."

Remember what I shared before, regarding our Armed Forces becoming POW's give Satan your name, rank, and serial number. I tell him, (out loud) "My name is _____ (insert your name), I am a child of God, my name is written in the Lamb's Book of Life. Look out, devil, you are under my feet. You are nothing to me. I belong to my Lord and Master, Jesus Christ.

CONFESSION: I am child of God!

PRAYER

Jesus, thank You so much for dying on the cross for my sins—all of my sins: past, present and future. I want my heart to be pure for You. I want to be used by You. I want to be like David, A man after

Your own heart. I ask you to remind me by your Holy Spirit to use the authority You gave me when the enemy tries to lasso me with condemnation. I know who I am; I am child of God. In Jesus' name, amen.

Day 35: Why Do You Trust Yourself?

Let no man say when he is tempted, I am tempted of God: for God cannot be tempted with evil, neither tempteth he any man: But every man is tempted, when he is drawn away of his own lust, and enticed. (James 1:13-14 KJV)

If there's one thing I don't understand when it comes to temptation and sin and trying to walk with God, it's why people put themselves in harm's way when it comes to the temptation of their flesh. Why do we trust ourselves?

It's like when somebody is on a diet, and they walk over to the dessert case or dessert menu pictures several times at the restaurant and stare at the carrot cake, lemon meringue pie, or strawberry shortcake. It doesn't make sense for you to do that; you are just tormenting yourself. Then there are the folks who should avoid sugar who consistently visit the candy and sweets stores.

Someone told me a story about when they worked at a gas station convenience store, and this Christian man said nothing bothers or tempts him anymore. (Do you sense pride here? I sure do.) To prove his point, he picked up a porn magazine and started to flip through the pages while saying, "See, that doesn't bother me anymore. I could go through all the magazines and stay strong." Wow. This leads me to the next scripture: "Wherefore let him that thinketh he standeth take heed lest he fall" (1 Corinthians 10:12 KJV).

If you know that you have a weakness (I sure do), keep yourself away from the thing that tempts you—period.

When temptation comes, you will typically be tempted with something that you feel you have been denied of or something that you feel you deserve. If you just finished a huge Thanksgiving Day meal with turkey, stuffing, cranberry sauce (the jelly in the can), and mashed potatoes, and someone offers you more turkey, the normal response would be, "Oh no, I'm stuffed." But wait about twenty minutes, and if they bring out some pumpkin pie with just the right amount of whipped cream, and your eyes bulge as you reach for it before they even ask if you want it.

A temptation is something you feel you really want, and you don't think about the consequences. What are the consequences? The Holy Spirit in you is grieved and saddened. You have disappointed Him. He feels a loss—and that loss is you. Your relationship has changed. Oh, He loves you and will always love you, so I am not talking about Him not loving you. But the relationship has been strained. You may ask what you can do to avoid this. Go to God. Go to the His throne room with boldness, and tell Him you need His mercy and grace and that you're sorry for hurting His feelings. It is important that you keep your relationship with Jesus "fresh."

What is the alternative to falling into temptation? ESCAPE IT!

> Submit yourselves therefore to God. Resist the devil, and he will flee from you. (James 4:7 KJV)

> There hath no temptation taken you but such as is common to man: but God is faithful, who will not suffer you to be tempted above that ye are able; but will with the temptation also make a way to escape, that ye may be able to bear it. (1 Corinthians 10:13 KJV)

There's always a way out if you look for it. Stop staring at the things you don't have, and fix your eyes on Jesus, the champion of your soul, and He will rescue you.

CONFESSION: I will resist temptation, in
Jesus' name!

PRAYER

I am so sorry, Jesus!

Day 36: Love Yourself

> Master, which is the great commandment in the law?
> Jesus said unto him, Thou shalt love the Lord thy God
> with all thy heart, and with all thy soul, and with all thy
> mind. This is the first and great commandment. And the
> second is like unto it, Thou shalt love thy neighbor **as
> thyself.** (Matthew 22:36-39 KJV)

As I woke up the other morning, this passage of scripture was laid on my heart. I recited it as I was contemplating getting out of bed. Then the Holy Spirit put an emphasis on the part, "thou shalt love they neighbor as thyself." He spoke to me and said, "My people need to learn to love themselves." Now that was as potent as three cups of coffee, and I shot out of bed!

First, allow me to cover the word *love.* Here is the Greek word *agape,* which is best described as unconditional love, the kind that expects nothing back. It is the highest form of love. Human love has limitations; God's love is unlimited. Agape love is the God-kind of love that He imparts into our spirit when we are born again.

So the greatest commandment tells us to love God with the love He put in us at the new birth, and with that same love, we are to *love ourselves.*

We are to love ourselves unconditionally. Let me ask you a couple of questions:

- Are you hard on yourself?
- Are you your worst critic?
- Do you find it easy to forgive others, but cannot find the grace to forgive yourself?

Maybe you messed up and blew it. You may have lost friends or maybe family over what you did. These are consequences for your actions and can be very difficult to walk through. You may have to deal with consequences for a while, but you have to reach deep within yourself to bring up that God-kind of love. Say to yourself, "I love you, and I forgive you."

The enemy will always try to remind you what you have done wrong. It's his job as the accuser of the brethren (Rev.12:10). Give yourself a break from the finger-pointing. Love yourself with the Holy Spirit. If you don't know how, just ask Him how to love yourself.

When you pray, try not to say, "Lord, what am I doing wrong?" Why? Well, it suggests that you are feeling guilty about something subconsciously. Instead, pray this: "Lord, what do You want me to do?" Don't allow the enemy to use your prayers against you.

Did you know it's okay to say no to others? It's okay to have healthy boundaries. Take some time off, pamper yourself. Get away with God. You can take the Holy Spirit with you to the gym and on holiday. He longs to spend time with you. You are important too. If you don't take care of yourself, you won't be able to help anyone else.

HOW TO LOVE YOURSELF: Receive Jesus, forgive yourself, forgive others quickly, and don't hold a grudge. Eat right physically and spiritually. Take care of your body and your soul. Read good books other than the Bible. Stay positive because you never know when you will need it. Keep your faith strong, even in challenging times. In closing, go see a therapist. Everyone's doing it now, so there's no need to be embarrassed. Or hire a life coach (There's a good one at www.GodStrength.Coach. com. I thought I would put a plug in!) God loves you, so love yourself!

CONFESSION: I will love myself today!

PRAYER

Father, in the name of Jesus, I need Your Holy Spirit today. Holy Spirit, I am asking You to walk and talk with me today. Show me how to love myself. Can You show me how to do this? Help me obey the greatest commandment. I know I can because You are living inside of me to help me. Amen!

Day 37: What If Jesus Compromised?

For I came down from heaven, not to do mine own will,
but the will of him that sent me. (John 6:38 KJV)

Our fearless leader had His mind made up, and His heart fixed on serving His heavenly Father. His example of living out His mission here on earth left us an inspiring lesson about living wholeheartedly for God with uncompromising determination.

Let's take a look at what the word *compromise* means, for it is quite revealing: "A settlement by arbitration or mutual consent reached by concessions on both sides."[5]

Keep in mind that you have already given your heart to God. You have decided to follow Jesus in every area of life that you operate in. The Father expects you to exhibit integrity in all of your business matters, in every conversation, and in your home life.

We get in trouble when we compromise on the will of the Father.

My question is: to whom and to what are you going to concede your integrity? Who are you talking to besides the Holy Spirit? Why would you be having a conversation from the dark side anyway? Have you settled on being worldly today in your behavior or thought processes? I strongly urge you to stop it—now.

If you have been compromising your Christian faith with the world, you will notice a lack of joy and confidence in your walk with God. The

5. Webster's Collegiate Dictionary, s.v. "Compromise," (G & C Merriam, Co: Springfield, MA, 1913).

contamination of the world is leaking in and diluting your morals through the crack of your compromise.

You may be thinking, *I know I have been compromising, but if I turn and start full throttle with the Lord and for His kingdom, won't I lose some of my friends?* Yes, and quite honestly, too bad! That's what you get for wandering into someone else's backyard. You have been walking the fence with one foot in the world and one foot in the kingdom of God. You lost your balance and fell off the fence. So just get back up, brush yourself off, put both of your hands to the plow, and don't look back.

I have never seen a happy backslider. They are always miserable. A fresh, vibrant walk with God awaits you today. A newborn godly disposition and countenance now rest on you, and others will take notice. It will bring the joy back and give you the strength to rid yourself of compromise until it comes to knock on the door of your heart again. So stay strong in the Lord and in the power of His might, and you will be ready.

Aren't you glad that Jesus never compromised? I sure am!

CONFESSION: I will do the will of the Father today!

PRAYER

Father God, I want You to know that I am so sorry for allowing compromise into my life. It has dampened my fire in our relationship, but as Your Word says, in 2 Timothy 1:6 (NLT), I will fan into flames the spiritual gift that God gave me. I stir up the gift of the Holy Spirit inside of me so I can burn with passion for You again. In Jesus' name, amen.

Day 38: The Spiritual Roadblock, Part 1

And Jesus said unto him, No man, having put his hand to the plough, and looking back, is fit for the kingdom of God. (Luke 9:62 KJV)

When a believer like yourself has locked both their hands to the plow of God's kingdom, wholeheartedly beginning to advance it, you become a significant threat to Satan's kingdom. Your determination has made you known in hell, and the spirits of darkness are waiting for the slightest crack to show in the door of your heart so they can claw their way into your life. Their mission is to stop any kind of forward motion in your life. One of satan's most powerful tools is something called condemnation.

To *condemn* is "to pronounce a sentence on (someone) in a court of law; demonstrate the guilt of (someone)."[6] *Condemnation* is defined as "The expression of strong disapproval; a final judgment of guilty in a criminal case and the punishment that is imposed."[7] Strong's Concordance says it means "to judge against, to sentence, to condemn and to damn."[8]

As you can see, it is a word you and I do not want anything to do with. Yet Satan and his demonic forces use condemnation very effectively. What's even more remarkable is that it is effective, both on the saved and on the unsaved—regardless of whether a person is strong in the Lord or not. That's because Satan knows that nothing will cause a person's life to come to a screeching halt more than condemnation.

---

6. Princeton University, "condemn," WordNet. Princeton University. 2010. Acessed 3 May, 2021. http://wordnetweb.princeton.edu/perl/webwn?s=condemn&sub=Search+WordNet&o2=&o0=1&o8=1&o1=1&o7=&o5=&o9=&o6=&o3=&o4=&h=.

7. Princeton University, "condemnation," WordNet. Princeton University. 2010. Accessed 3 May, 2021. http://wordnetweb.princeton.edu/perl/webwn?s=condemnation&sub=-Search+WordNet&o2=&o0=1&o8=1&o1=1&o7=&o5=&o9=&o6=&o3=&o4=&h=000000.

8. "G4103 - pistos - Strong's Greek Lexicon (KJV)." Blue Letter Bible. Accessed 3 May, 2021. https://www.blueletterbible.org//lang/lexicon/lexicon.cfm?Strongs=G4103&t=KJV.

Let's say that you're driving, and in the distance, you see police lights and begin to wonder if there was an accident or something? As you drive closer, you realize that it is a police roadblock. Your heart jumps, wondering if you're late for your vehicle inspection or you left your license at home. The next thought you have is to turn off the road and go a different way—but the police are smarter than you, and they've positioned themselves where there is no street to turn off onto. The roadblock was cleverly designed this way, and now you're trapped. You now await the dreaded voice of the officer, saying, "Please pull over to the curb."

Even if you have nothing to be worried about, your mind still races to make sure you have dotted every *i* and crossed every *t* of every road law possible. Then a sigh of relief comes when you realize that your car has been inspected, you have your license, your seatbelt is on, and you have no warrants out for your arrest. You roll down the window, look right into the face of the police officer, smile, and offer up a "have a nice day" as he waves you back on your journey. A great feeling, isn't it?

It's also great to know that now there is no condemnation for those who belong to Christ Jesus (Romans 8:1). There is *no* condemnation, and anyone who blows a whistle, points at you to pull over, and tries to tell you that your walk with God is over is simply a great big fat liar!

CONFESSION: No one condemns me anymore!

PRAYER

Father, thank You for lifting the yoke that condemnation puts on me. You said Your yoke is easy, and Your burden is light. I want to learn and understand that Your righteousness is upon my life. It is my breastplate, and I wear it proudly in Jesus' name, amen.

Day 39: The Spiritual Roadblock, Part 2

And Jesus said unto him, No man, having put his hand to the plough, and looking back, is fit for the kingdom of God. (Luke 9:62 KJV)

Several years ago I recorded a series about condemnation. To my surprise, the CD cover designer put a picture of a dog on it. I was puzzled by the artwork, so I called her and asked, "What's up with the dog on the front?" I loved her response. She said it wasn't a dog but rather a hyena. I was intrigued and asked her to explain. She told me that one of the traits of a hyena, other than having a hideous laugh and powerful jaws, is they come back repeatedly for a kill. They hunt and haunt their prey relentlessly, leading it to give up, thinking it has failed. This is very similar to our experience of condemnation; we are relentlessly pursued by thoughts of failure, that we are useless to God, and that He will never forgive us—and we become prey to the hideous laugh of condemnation.

Churches are supposed to be places where everyone should be built up and encouraged. However, condemnation finds its roots embedded in the foundation of religion. It raises up its horns, and will thrust them into anyone who doesn't have the revelation of God's grace. Condemnation is a roadblock set by Satan, and he wants you to believe there is no escape from it, that we can no longer move forward in God and that any spiritual momentum we once had is gone. Thankfully, we can go directly to the Judge to get permission to move ahead.

Let us, therefore, come boldly unto the throne of grace, that we may obtain mercy, and find grace to help in time of need. (Hebrews 4:16 KJV)

If you have found yourself in a situation where you compromised or fell, the enemy is probably screaming at you that you are no good and will never amount to anything. You need to be very aware of this truth: the voice of condemnation is always lying because he is a liar; he is the father of lies (John 8:44)!

Condemnation that is not dealt with can become a stronghold in your life. I was brought up Catholic, and I tried to be a very good one. I was taught that when you sin, you must confess it to a priest (a man), and he would give absolution and then give you a penance. Now *penance* is a real eye-opener. It means "a means of obtaining the remission of sins by the performance of expiatory rites, voluntary submission to punishment."[9] You might recognize it as saying three "Hail Marys" and three "Our Fathers."

But we don't have to do any of those things. Jesus already died for all of our sins on the cross—PERIOD. All of our sins: past, present, and future. ALL!

Before you read through the next passage, I would like to point out the word *now*. It is an adverb that means "the present time or moment."[10] So at this present time—at this precise moment—condemnation has no power over you.

> Therefore, there is now no condemnation for those who are in Christ Jesus, because through Christ Jesus the law of the Spirit who gives life has set you free from the law of sin and death. (Romans 8:1-2 NIV)

CONFESSION: I will not frustrate the grace of God!

---

9. Webster's Collegiate Dictionary, s.v. "penance," (G & C Merriam, Co: Springfield, MA, 1913).
10. Webster's Collegiate Dictionary, s.v. "now," (G & C Merriam, Co: Springfield, MA, 1913).

PRAYER

Father, in Jesus' name, I receive the forgiveness that comes with the shed blood at Calvary. By the grace of God I will not allow Satan, others, or even myself, to speak the voice of condemnation into my heart. I remove the spiritual roadblock, In Jesus' name, amen.

Day 40: He Raised You Up

The Lord God is my strength, and he will make my feet like hinds' feet, and he will make me walk upon my high places. (Habakkuk 3:19 KJV)

I am so inspired by a song that the Celtic Women sing entitled "You Raise Me Up."

I believe it is one of my favorite songs. It is simply lovely and powerfully inspirational. I associate it with my relationship with God. Through this relationship I have with my Savior, my Master, my Lord, is where I receive the GodStrength necessary for me to accomplish my assignment or overcome anything here on earth. God's Spirit has that incredible ability to raise us up and open our eyes to receive His perspective in a situation.

This is very similar to what Habakkuk wrote above. Mountain goats are built like climbing machines. Their hard hooves give them the ability to dig or kick away debris. Their hooves also are split for balance, and the soft parts work like Velcro, enabling them to stick to stone surfaces. They can ascend up to twelve feet in a single jump. This is what the Lord can do within us in just a moment. But we must believe and never give up. We must tap into this GodStrength for our sake and for those in our lives.

David had similar experiences:

For thou wilt light my candle: the Lord my God will enlighten my darkness. For by thee I have run through a troop, and by my God have I leaped over a wall. (Psalms 18:28-29 KJV)

See, that's GodStrength being imparted! The good news is that it's for us too.

So come on up to the high place of His presence, His perspective, His knowledge, and His strength. It can happen instantly or over time. Once I make the decision to seek Him wholeheartedly, something changes inside of me. Let's make a decision together right now. Let's make the following confession:

CONFESSION: I am going up to the high place of His presence today!

PRAYER

Lord, I am so sorry, for I have made You too small in my eyes. You are bigger, larger, and more powerful than the problem or situation I am dealing with. Mountain: be removed in Jesus's name, and if you do not remove yourself, God will simply give me the strength to climb you and overtake you with Christ's perspective. In Jesus' name, amen.

Day 41: No One Crashes and Burns in a Day

> They went out from us, but they were not of us; for if they had been of us, they would no doubt have continued with us: but they went out, that they might be made manifest that they were not all of us. (1 John 2:19 KJV)

The scripture above talks about the spirit of antichrist attacking the body of Christ, and it explicitly explains that those people were never truly with them.

Have you ever known of someone who you thought was saved and later fell away? Maybe it was a man or woman of God or a godly family that seemed like they had it all together, but later you heard that they left the church, left their spouse, or robbed a bank or something crazy like that. You probably thought, *How did that happen?* Be very aware that no one crashes and burns in a day!

Though all of them looked good in the natural: showed up for church, sang in the choir, and even paid their tithe—something was happening in the background of their life. The garden of their life looked really good, but grubs, destructive insects, and groundhogs were burrowing underneath their veneer life.

So when you see and hear about Christians who have fallen, do not judge them, but love them, and if applicable, allow God to use you to restore them. But do not be surprised anymore.

How about you? Are you allowing what the writer of Song of Solomon 2:15 is talking about when he refers to the "little foxes spoiling the vine?" It's the little things that will take you down; it's a slow fade, not a crash and burn. I am sure we have experienced this in our own life, but others didn't know it at the time. They thought you were just sad or having a bad day, but we knew better, didn't we. Again, there's no judgment here, but we must take responsibility for our actions—both outward and hidden. How do we do this?

- Step one: accept the **responsibility** of deciding to do the right thing.
- Second, **believe** that God has provided you the power to do so.

You must be **determined** in your heart to obey your calling, and God will empower you. By the Spirit of God, every individual can perform their calling with excellence.

Allow me to share two scriptures with you. Many people will stop after reading the first one. They wish they could be a vessel of honor like their favorite pastor or teacher, but they just don't think they qualify. Let's read:

> But in a great house, there are not only vessels of gold and of silver, but also of wood and of earth; and some to honor, and some to dishonor.

Now, this is where you come in:

> If a man, therefore, purge himself from these, he shall be a vessel unto honor, sanctified, and meet for the master's use, and prepared unto every good work. (2 Timothy 2:20-21 KJV)

As you can see, it's your choice. No one crashes and burns in a day; it's a choice, so choose wisely today.

CONFESSION; I am a child of God and a servant of the Most High God!

PRAYER

Father, forgive me for allowing the little foxes to come into my garden and nibble at the vine of our connection. Help me to remove them, in Jesus' name, amen.

Day 42: Wrong Thinking vs. Thinking Wrong Things

Do not conform to the pattern of this world, but be transformed by the renewing of your mind. Then you will be able to test and approve what God's will is—his good, pleasing, and perfect will. (Romans 12:2 NIV)

Allow me to clarify what I mean by the above statement. This will help you understand what I am trying to impart today.

Wrong thinking is bad thinking because the thought process doesn't line up with the philosophy of the Word of God, but rather, the world.

Thinking wrong things is also bad, but not as harmful. Both can and must be changed, but wrong thinking will take longer to change because it has a stronghold on us unless, of course, God brings deliverance to our mind.

We are encouraged not to conform our thinking after the pattern of the world or worldly people. However, He instructs us to renew our minds to line up with the mind of Christ that He put in us (our spirit) at the new birth. The incentive to do so is that we will be able to test and approve what God's will is for our life.

Worldly thinking will never understand the will of God.

Wrong thinking has to do with strongholds and can come in the form of first-impulse responses. I don't know about you, but my first impulses are not always good. They also can be addictions or thoughts that hinder us from believing who we really are, who we belong to, and what we are called to do. So these must be removed, for they limit us.

(For the weapons of our warfare are not carnal, but mighty through God to the pulling down of strongholds;) Casting down imaginations, and every high thing that exalteth itself against the knowledge of God, and bringing into captivity every thought to the obedience of Christ. (2 Corinthians 10:4-5 KJV)

"Every high thing that exalteth itself against the knowledge of God" must come down! It is demonic, it is worldly—and it is hindering you.

I was intrigued when I saw what *high things* meant in Greek. The Strongs Concordance says it's an elevated place or thing in our mind, or an altitude and a barrier.[11] When I saw the word *barrier* I thought, *Wow*!

The enemy, the low-life devil, used the trauma, abuse, and bad things we experienced throughout our lifetime, and put a barrier in our thought process to stop us from becoming what God intended for us. What a snake!

The good news is that the Holy Spirit is revealing something to you right now. He has the ability and power to destroy the works of the devil.

I hope you're ready to fight the good fight of faith. God is not in your corner—He is living and breathing inside of you. Know it and flow in it, and watch the barriers come down. With every barrier that comes down, God's will for your life is revealed more and more.

CONFESSION: Jesus is lifted high, and strongholds are coming down!

---

11. "G5313 - hypsōma - Strong's Greek Lexicon (KJV)." Blue Letter Bible. Accessed 3 May, 2021. https://www.blueletterbible.org//lang/lexicon/lexicon.cfm?Strongs=G5313&t=KJV.

PRAYER

Lord, thank You for this eye-opener. The trickster, the enemy, the snake, has planted a barrier in my mind. I commit myself to renew my mind, and I come against every high thing, every barrier-thought that the enemy has used to hinder me is coming down. The will of God is my heart's desire, and I am closer to hearing more of it now, in Jesus' name, amen.

Day 43: What You Think of Yourself Matters

For as he thinketh in his heart, so is he. (Proverbs 23:7 KJV)

This is a very interesting scripture that poses a question: What do you think of yourself?

Does it really matter what you think of yourself? It matters a great deal because how we think of ourselves is who we become, even if it's a lie. So we must learn to see ourselves as God's sees us. This is a good follow-up to yesterday's devotional about wrong thinking.

Are your thoughts about yourself limiting you? They are if you don't view yourself as God sees you.

Who do you see when you look into a mirror? Do you see the real you, or do you see someone you don't like? Someone who looks out of place or with a bad image? I am not talking about accepting yourself or trying to see yourself as a celebrity or sports star; I'm talking about seeing the *real you*, and knowing that you are true to your morals and values.

I assume you are a believer if you have gotten this far into the devotional. You must have morals, standards, and values that probably line up with the Bible. If you're not living according to your standards, morals, or values, then you are really living someone else's life and not being true to the believer in you.

Let's take a look at a story in the Bible where people thought less of themselves. Twelve spies were sent in to check out the land of Cannan that God told them to go and possess. They came back with this story:

126

But the men that went up with him said, We be not able to go up against the people; for they are stronger than we. And they brought up an evil report of the land which they had searched unto the children of Israel, saying, The land, through which we have gone to search it, is a land that eateth up the inhabitants thereof; and all the people that we saw in it are men of great stature. And there we saw the giants, the sons of Anak, which come of the giants: **and we were in our own sight as grasshoppers, and so we were in their sight**. (Numbers 13:31-33 KJV)

Ten of the spies came back and said, "We were in our own sight as grasshoppers." Wow! What a distorted way to look at yourself: "I look like a bug." This is why we need God's perspective of our own lives.

For you to accomplish what you are called to do, you need to see yourself as who God created you to be. What does that look like? In His image and likeness. Ten of the spies saw themselves as insects—so contrary to who they were. They were children of the Most High God. They were God's chosen people to take the land. They were people who had faith in a mighty powerful God, yet for some reason, it was distorted.

I think that they were living a lower life than what God called them to. They lived with a negative mindset that was contrary to the character and person of the God they served. They may have been living under the radar of their true morals, values, and truths they were raised in, and because of that, it distorted who they were. If you are living below the standard of excellence you have set for yourself, when you look in a mirror, your values and morales will cause you to see a reflection which is less of the person you really are.

CONFESSION: I see myself as a champion!

PRAYER

Lord, I am so sorry for distorting the image You created me to be. I repent of the low standards I have set for myself. My morals, values, and truth for life is supposed to line up with Your thoughts, Your ways, and Your Word. Thank You so much for this revelation. In Jesus' name, amen.

Day 44: God-Fidence

Being confident of this very thing, that he which hath begun a good work in you will perform it until the day of Jesus Christ. (Philippians 1:6 KJV)

This passage has been a blessing to me many times over the years. It's like celebrating the new year every time I read and believe it.

In the year 2000, I underwent brain surgery to remove a pituitary tumor from behind my eyes. It was crushing my optic nerve, and I was losing my peripheral vision slowing each day without even realizing it. I am thankful that the tumor was benign, but it did put me through some emotional turmoil.

To make a long story short, I went through a six-hour operation where the doctor went up my nose with a rubber hose. I was blind, and now I see. Any time your brain is messed with, who knows what would happen.

Emotionally, I was off the charts. The pituitary gland is a major gland which controls most of the regulation of hormones in the body. So when dealing with removal of that gland, whether you're male or female, one's hormones can either soar or crash. After the operation, I seemed to have lost my bearings. One day in desperation, I preached a message to my wife at the kitchen table which I entitled, "I've Got to Be Me." Jean was so nervous seeing me this way. Recovering physically was okay, but emotionally, it was challenging.

One day I was sitting in my reading chair and I came across today's passage and I stopped at it. I read it over and over again. Then I stood up and confessed it out loud. Something was happening to me. Walls were coming down! I felt so drawn to God at that moment. I was shouting and praising God as healing was manifesting in me. I was filled (here it is!) with GODFIDENCE.

Maybe you're going through an emotional trial or circumstance and you thinking of quitting, going back into the world, or getting drunk, losing your faith in yourself, God, or others. Perhaps you are contemplating major decisions such as closing a business or something on a larger scale. I would urge you not to do anything until you get your GODFIDENCE BACK.

Philippians 1:6 is a breath of fresh air for any situation you may be found dealing with or that you've gotten yourself into. Whether it was your fault or someone else's doesn't matter. God is not a respecter of persons; but He is a respecter of faith. Read this verse:

> But without faith, it is impossible to please him: for he that cometh to God must believe that he is and that he is a rewarder of them that diligently seek him. (Hebrews 11:6 KJV)

I challenge you to make a move toward God and submit to Him and His loving care and power. He promises that if you draw close to Him, He will draw close to you. He will meet you just like He met me at my reading chair. When I began confessing my GODFIDENCE in Him, He was able to help me perform and finish the work that He started in me. It's your turn now!

CONFESSION: We can do this, God!

PRAYER

Father God, you know where I'm at. You know the situation of my life and the circumstances I face. Alone, I am a goner, but with You, I am a winner. I draw close to you now, Lord, with full anticipation of a transfer of GodStrength. When I am confident that You are for me, then who can seriously be against me? No one. Father, I receive my GODFIDENCE and release it into my situation. In Jesus' name, amen.

Day 45: Karma?

Be not over much wicked, neither be thou foolish: why shouldest thou die before thy time? (Ecclesiastes 7:17 KJV)

M any years ago I had an outreach center in a poor neighborhood that was close to an elementary school. One day I read in the news that a young boy who attended the school skipped class and climbed up on the roof of the school. Unfortunately, he lost his footing, fell through the skylight in the roof, and plunged to his death. I was quite saddened to read about a young boy carelessly losing his life in a moment of disobedience. This story is what comes to my mind whenever I read this passage. I have no doubt that the young boy died before his time. But it didn't have to happen.

I do not believe in karma, which is a major belief in Hinduism, Ayyavazhi, Sikhism, Buddhism, and Jainism, that basically says that your future existence is determined by the sum of your actions

I believe that people reap what they sow. When we do things consistently that we know is contrary to a godly lifestyle, we are putting ourselves at risk. You can be in the wrong place at the wrong time. It has happened to many. But walking in wisdom can position us to be in the right place at the right time more often than not.

Look at this passage:

> Do not be deceived: God cannot be mocked. A man reaps what he sows. Whoever sows to please their flesh, from the flesh will reap destruction; whoever sows to please the Spirit, from the Spirit will reap eternal life. Let us not become weary in doing good, for at the proper time

132

we will reap a harvest if we do not give up. Therefore, as we have the opportunity, let us do good to all people, especially to those who belong to the family of believers. (Galatians 6:7-10 NIV)

Have you ever heard someone say (usually with a laugh) "If I knew I would have lived this long, I would have taken better care of myself." I say, "How dumb can you get and still breathe?"

If you are eating things you shouldn't, drinking and getting drunk, playing around, sinning and living any old way you want, please know that it will catch up with you. You could come down with a disease, a sickness, or get in trouble with the law. I don't believe you will always reap what you sow in regard to sinning. Thank God that Jesus died for your sins, but the foolishness of continuing in sin will catch up with you eventually: AIDS, high blood pressure, cancer of the throat, a broken marriage with a stranger raising your children—all because you resisted the Holy Spirit when He cautioned you. If you continue to refuse to conform to God's ways, my advice is to keep your eyes open for that skylight!

CONFESSION: God, I will obey You today!

PRAYER

Lord, I love You with all of my heart, but there are days when my head gets in the way. Pressures of life rush in, and I begin to lose my balance. I am asking You, Holy Spirit, to remind me of this story because I want a good ending to my life. In Jesus' name, amen.

Day 46: A Benefit of Following Jesus

So he left that area, and many people followed him. He healed all the sick among them. (Matthew 12:15 NLT)

This is my first devotional I have written in several weeks after coming off one of the biggest trials and near-death experiences of my life. I returned from England three weeks ago and woke up with the Covid-19 virus in my lungs. I suffered from extreme fatigue, so I slept, slept, and slept. I only woke up occasionally to use the restroom or to get something small to eat.

After five days of the extreme fatigue, I tested positive for the virus. I got a phone call that said, "You are positive for the Coronavirus. Please free to go to the hospital if you wish. Do not feel silly or that you are over-reacting. Lastly they said, "If there are any changes, keep us informed."

I hung up and just sat there, stunned and wondering where it had come from. (we all know it came from hell, but now I had to deal with it.) Unfortunately, after sleeping for five days, I didn't feel like a spiritual giant; more like a gnat. Sorry to disappoint you, but I'm not your hero in this. Jesus is your hero. Jesus is my hero.

It wasn't too much longer until I noticed my breathing began to be short, and I would pant more than breathe. I remembered what the voice on the other end of the phone said about not being afraid to call an ambulance.

I was taken to the hospital and my world instantly became darker. I was placed into a COVID-19 center that looked more like a sci-fi movie scene with nurses and doctors wrapped in medical protection gear. They assaulted me with question after question, and I couldn't remember all

134

the facts. After all, I had been asleep for five days and was extremely fatigued. I was out of it!

I do remember when the big question was asked: "Do you want to be resuscitated?" I paused a moment at the question and thought to myself, *My goodness; it has come to this?* I know it's a routine question for them to ask, but it was not a routine moment for me. I responded with a resounding, "Yes, of course, I want to be resuscitated." That ended the questions.

I began to lean on nothing but the thought of Jesus my Savior and Lord. No, I didn't instantly become a spiritual giant of a man, but rather a man who simply needed God.

The good news is that I made it home, and at the time of this writing, I am in isolation. My experience has drawn me closer to God than ever. My first day home, I read today's scripture, and it just jumped off the page. It said to me: Just keep following Jesus, and as you follow Him, He will heal you. I know that's not an exact quotation, but is how God used it to speak to me. Wherever you at, whatever you're going through, my advice is this: FOLLOW JESUS!

CONFESSION: I will follow Jesus where ever i go!

PRAYER

Father God, thank You so much for Your healing power and for Your love for us. Even when we are flat on our back, sicker than a dog, You still have us covered. Thank You so much for the investment You put in me. I pray You will get a mighty return. And, Lord, by the way, thank You for resuscitating me. in Jesus' name, amen.

Day 47: Standing At the Door of Faith

And at even, when the sun did set, they brought unto him
all that were diseased, and them that were possessed with
devils. And all the city was gathered together at the door.
(Mark 1:32-33 KJV)

This is a massive testimony of people following Jesus and being healed,
set free, and delivered. The amazing part is that it says, "And **all
the city was gathered together at the door**." I know my heart would be
pounding with excitement if I was either inside the house with Jesus or
right at the doorway looking into the house. It must have been electrify-
ing, to say the least. One person would leave praising and glorifying God,
and another would walk through the door. People were pressing into the
kingdom of God.

The attraction that Jesus had, matched the anointing that God put on Him.
Act 2:38 (KJV) says, "God anointed Jesus of Nazareth with the Holy Ghost
and with power, who went about doing good healing all that were oppressed
of the devil: for God was with Him."

When I read that the whole city was standing at the door, I always think
of it as the door of faith. My reasoning comes from Ephesians 6:16, "Above
all, taking the shield of faith, wherewith ye shall be able to quench all the
fiery darts of the wicked."

The Greed word for *shield* refers to a large shield (like a door-shaped
shield) which comes from a root word that means a portal or entrance.

Faith is the portal we must enter so we can please God. Faith is the
entrance for our miracle. The shield of faith is a door-shaped shield, or the

entrance or the portal to the supernatural where we can receive our miracles, our blessing, or our healings.

When we enter this portal or door of faith it creates a protective shield around us. It shields us by giving us the ability to quench all the fiery darts (lies and schemes) that satan throws at us. It makes them bounce off of us as we move forward toward the promises God has for us.

There are times when it seems the odds are against us. But these are the time we must press through the door of faith to advance the kingdom of God in our lives and into the lives of others.

I think of this scripture in regard to pressing in:

> And from the time John the Baptist began preaching until now, the Kingdom of Heaven has been forcefully advancing, and violent people are attacking it. (Matthew 11:12 NLT)

We have to be forcefully advancing. Why? Because we have opposition, whether its satan, our flesh, or others. We must go through the door of faith.

The next verse gives us a glimpse into what happened when people went through the door of faith and if we continue.

> And he healed many that were sick of divers diseases, and cast out many devils; and suffered not the devils to speak, because they knew him. (Mark 1:34 KJV)

CONFESSION: I am going to be an enforcer for the kingdom of God!

PRAYER

Father God, Thank You for the faith You have given me to believe in You. Thank You for the ability to walk through the door of faith and to be able to quench every lie, scheme, and trick of the enemy. All your promises are yes and amen, and, Lord, I pray for the tenacity, the consistency, and the passion to move forward. In Jesus' name, amen.

Day 48: Do You Need a Haircut?

Howbeit the hair of his head began to grow again after he was shaven. (Judges 16:22 KJV)

If you have not read this whole story of Samson, I encourage you to read it; it's a great one! This passage excites me. Right now most of the world can relate to needing a haircut. It's the year 2020 in New York, USA, and we are in a lockdown. Just about every man, woman, and child needs a haircut at this point in time. Unfortunately, nobody knows when hairdressers will open up again so it doesn't look like it will happen anytime soon—unless you trust your sister to cut it.

Allow me to pose a question to you: Are you getting ahold of God during this time off?

Sampson made a huge mistake in his life and as a result, his enemy plucked his eyes out and made him walk in circles grinding wheat; which a donkey would do. Every day was the same and I'm sure it reached the point of monotony for him.

Are you feeling that way now? Have you failed, let people down, or has this lockdown, shut down, shelter in—or whatever you want to call it—beginning to feel like a grind? As you go through the grind of life, you have to protect your thought life because you're starting to think thoughts that are contrary to what you really believe. The monotony may be beginning to wear on you, causing you to believe lies that say God has forgotten about you, you are going to be in financial ruin, you are going to die, nobody loves you, or nobody cares. Please know God loves you very much, and He knows exactly where you are and what you need.

Can you imagine the guilt, condemnation, and rejection that must have been flooding Sampson's mind as he walked every day in his boring, ho-hum life around the grind? I have good news. Something was happening behind the scenes that no one anticipated to be a problem. What am I talking about? Hair!

Sampson's hair began to grow again. It is more about Sampson's deep commitment to God rather than the natural process of his hair growing. His hair was just a symbol of his commitment to God, which was the secret to his strength, just like your strength comes from God when you believe on Him.

Sampson must have been thinking, meditating, and praying to His God as he walked the grind every day. Are you? Are you using this time to get strong in the Lord and in the power of His might? Or are you just sitting on your laurels and binge-watching TV shows or movies?

I highly encourage you to find the **will of God** for your life in this season. Don't waste valuable time just playing games, eating, drinking, or doing drugs. Get ahold of God. Use this time to bond with your spouse, your children, friends, and loved ones.

Maybe you are asking, "Lord, what is going on. What should I do?" Consider this:

> That they (you) should seek the Lord, if haply they might feel after him, and find him, though he is not far from every one of us: For in him we live, and move, and have our being. (Acts 17:27-28 KJV)

So do you need a haircut? You aren't alone. Do you need to get a hold of God? Guess what. You are not alone there either. Let us grow together.

CONFESSION: Lord, my hair is growing!

PRAYER

Father, in the name of Jesus, I ask You to draw me close to You in this hour. You promised, Lord, that if I draw close to You, You will draw near to me. I recognize that this is a season of getting ahold of You, Lord. For in You I live and move and have my being. Amen.

Day 49: I Will Die for You, Lord, and Will Never Deny You

Peter said unto him, Though I should die with thee, yet will I not deny thee. Likewise also said all the disciples. (Matthew 26:35 KJV)

Peter seems to have been a very passionate man. He is known by preachers as the man with the "foot-shaped" mouth. Why? Because he always seemed to put his foot in his mouth by not thinking before he spoke. Trust me, I can relate to him personally when it comes to what I call "foot-in-mouth disease."

I want to point out that Peter wasn't the only one who made this rash confession. It says, "likewise also said all the disciples." Peter was a leader, and, unfortunately, leaders are not perfect but human—and being human means having flaws.

I believe Peter was very sincere in his declaration, the problem was that he wasn't in a position to make this type of declaration due to a lack of consecration in his life. He was a young follower in Christ and He (like us) had a lot to learn. After making this statement he got a good education, and trust me, he finished the course and gave his life for his Savior.

Tradition teaches that Peter was killed on a cross like Jesus, but he requested to be hung upside down because he didn't consider himself to be worthy to be crucified as His Lord was. It has been said that he was crucified alongside his wife, and the whole time he kept comforting his wife by saying, "Remember the Lord. Remember the Lord."

When Peter denied the Lord, it was a traumatic experience. When we sin, do we look into the eyes of Jesus like he did? Look at this:

> And Peter said, Man, I know not what thou sayest. And immediately, while he yet spake, the cock crew. **And the Lord turned and looked upon Peter**. And Peter remembered the word of the Lord, how he had said unto him, Before the cock crow, thou shalt deny me thrice. And Peter went out, and wept bitterly. (Luke 22:60-62 KJV)

No wonder Peter ran out and wept bitterly! Peter didn't have the maturity, level of commitment, or consecration necessary, or the Holy Spirit to help him. The Holy Spirit was not poured out until Pentecost, which is when Peter roared like a lion and preached up a storm. Along with Peter, the apostles, disciples, and even the Lord's mother, Mary, were in the upper room hiding in fear. Then the Holy Ghost filled them with courage and power.

God's Holy Spirit is the game-changer, and He is available to fill you if you so desire. We need the Holy Spirit to guide us in every area of our life. We also need Him for the GodStrength we need to live for Him. That is the reason for this devotional: To live for Him.

I consider myself a bold Christian. I say that humbly and without a chip on my shoulder. When I first got saved, I worked in a factory. There was a lovely religious man there. I will call him John. John had incredible strength. He would shake men's hands and squeeze them till the men fell on his knees and pleaded with him to let go. I know this because he did it to me.

One day John approached me with what he thought was a powerful confession of his faith. He said: "What if I told you that I would give my right arm to Jesus." I boldly looked him in the eye with love and compassion and said, "Keep your stinking arm; He wants your life!"

143

CONFESSION: "If we died with Him, we will also live with him." (2 Timothy 2:11 NIV)

PRAYER

Father, thank You for giving uo Your life for me. You have shown me the way. I may not have to ever die for You, but If I will learn to die out to this life so I can truly live for You. In Jesus' name, amen.

Day 50: What Were the Last Words Jesus Said to You before the Storm?

And the same day, when the even was come, he saith unto them, Let us pass over unto the other side. (Mark 4:35 KJV)

I heard a preacher speak about this, and God used it to ushered the word of faith into my life. If you're not familiar with the word of faith, it's when you hear the Word of God and you believe it to be the word that God is giving to help you, guide you, or empower you through any circumstance. It's God speaking directly to you about your given situation and giving you faith for a good outcome.

Jesus said, "Let us pass over unto the other side." In this passage, they were crossing the Sea of Galilee. Unfortunately for them, a powerful storm rose up. They were experienced fishermen and were trained to be out at sea, but this storm was different. It was threatening their lives. They were terrified and thought they were going to die. What really baffled them was the fact that Jesus, their Master, was on the boat with them, and He didn't seem to care about their dire situation. He was relaxing, sleeping with His head on a pillow as the waves rocked Him to sleep.

I wonder if they dared each other to wake Jesus up. They may have be afraid of Him, but more afraid of dying. So they all got around Him and yelled, "Master, carest thou not that we perish?" (Mark 4:38 KJV)

And he arose, and rebuked the wind, and said unto the sea, Peace, be still. And the wind ceased, and there was a great calm. And he said unto them, Why are ye so fearful? how is it that ye have no faith? (Mark 4:39-40 KJV)

Watch now:

> And they feared exceedingly, and said one to another,
> What manner of man is this, that even the wind and the
> sea obey him? (Mark 4:41 KJV)

I tend to read stories and see the humor in it, and this story makes me laugh! I'm sure I would have acted the same was as the disciples did if I was on that boat. But the human emotion must have been off the charts.

Lets zoom in on the purpose of this devotional. Why did Jesus ask, "Why are you so fearful? How is it that ye have no faith?"

So forget about the storm at sea for a moment. Let's go back and see what Jesus said to them before they even got into the boat. He said, "Let us pass over to the other side." Jesus meant what He said, and He had plans to wake up and be on the other side of the lake. He knew what He said, He meant what He said, and He expected it to come to pass!

So what did God say to you before you went through your storm? He doesn't change His mind about your destiny, your dream, or the plan He gave you for your future. Don't allow the storms of life to diminish the power of the Word of God that was spoken to you.

What did God say to you before you got sick? Before your house burned down? Before your child backslid? You have to remember these things— because what He spoke to you was meant to encourage you to never give up on your dream, marriage, family, or destiny. "For no word from God will ever fail" (Luke 1:37 NIV).

CONFESSION: I will make it to the other side of this storm!

PRAYER

Jesus, first of all, I want to tell You that I am so sorry for doubting You. I'm going to take the words You speak to me and cherish them close to my heart. David said, "Thy word is a lamp unto my feet, and a light unto my path." I believe in Your Word, Lord. In Jesus' name, amen.

Day 51: Mr. Lonely

But Jesus often withdrew to lonely places and prayed.
(Luke 5:16 NIV)

P rayer is the transfer of God's strength. I recommend taking the time
to study the prayer life of Jesus Christ. I believe His example would
be very inspirational for you.

When I was battling COVID-19, the Holy Spirit impressed upon
me to take inventory of my devotional life. When I did, I realized that
I came up short—not just in the length of my prayer, but in depth. That
well of bubbling water in me was being stifled with the debris of my
busy ministry life.

I thought I was on top of my world. It's like 1 Corinthians 10:12
(NLT) says, "If you think you stand, be careful not to fall." Well, I didn't
fall far, but I fell into sickness. But God, in His mercy and grace, healed
me and the Holy Spirit revealed His goodness to me. Then that precious
well of water began to bubble up again, and it drew me into a fresh new
prayer life.

Jesus loved praying in mountains, in gardens, and just about anyplace
he could sneak off to just to talk to His Father. As the scripture above
says, He even withdrew to lonely places to pray.

He prayed in the morning:

> And in the morning, rising up a great while before day,
> he went out and departed into a solitary place, and there
> prayed. (Mark 1:35 KJV)

That is impressive to me because I am not a morning person. But how do we know if Jesus was? We don't know. Prayer is always a sacrifice.

Jesus prayed when the sun went down:

> And it came to pass in those days, that he went out into a mountain to pray, and continued all night in prayer to God. (Luke 6:12 KJV)

He also prayed in the afternoon:

> And when he had sent the multitudes away, he went up into a mountain apart to pray: and when the evening came, he was there alone. (Matthew 14:23 KJV)

Jesus didn't go up to the mountain in the dark, but in the afternoon and began to pray and when the sun went down he stayed to pray all night. His disciples took notice that after Jesus spent time in prayer, He worked miracles. The blind could see, the deaf could hear and the dead were raised. The disciples never once asked Jesus to teach them how to heal the sick or raise the dead; but they did ask, "Lord, teach us to pray, just as John taught his disciples" (Luke 11:1).

Consider asking the Holy Spirit when is the best time for you to pray. If you are reading this, then I assume you have a daily devotional time, and finding the best time to pray will be important to you. With the little experience I have in time management, I found it best for myself to write down a to-do list for the day, and then do the hardest things first. I'm not saying prayer or devotions are hard, but what I have found is that if I don't do devotions prayer as soon as possible, it can become hard to find the time as the day passes.

Why pray? Prayer is how we communicate with God. God wants you to talk to Him in your own language and accent. You can cry, weep, and complain, but also give Him praise, honor, and thanks. You will ask Him for things and to help others. God also wants to speak to you. In the book of Revelation it is written seven times, "He that hath an ear let him hear what the Spirit is saying to the church." The Holy Spirit wants us to hear what He has to say. So find a lonely place and pray!

CONFESSION: Flesh, you are going to pray today!

PRAYER

Holy Spirit, bring me into Your presence every single day. In Jesus' name, amen.

Day 52: Don't Leave Too Soon or You Could Arrive Powerless

But they that wait upon the Lord shall renew their strength; they shall mount up with wings as eagles; they shall run, and not be weary; and they shall walk, and not faint. (Isaiah 40:31 KJV)

Many of us have a really hard time when we have to wait. We live in a generation where many people have the attention span of a gerbil. It may have happened when the TV remote was invented and we had the ability to change the channel with one click. Then, of course, cable TV arrives with hundreds of channels to choose from, and then we sit there and click, click, click, etc.

Waiting can be difficult in the world we live in. But if you desire to walk in the power of the spirit, know the will of God, and hear from God what to do in a given situation, then I highly recommend that you learn to wait upon the Lord—and don't do anything or go anywhere until you do!

When you wait upon the Lord, you create an opportunity for the transfer of GodStrength to be imparted into you. That's God's Strength in you and through you. So spend time with the Lord before you purchase that expensive car, house, or any other big ticket item.

Wait upon the Lord:

- With your spouse before making a big decision
- Before going into business

- Before you date or get engaged
- Before you step out in faith to do something really big or costly
- To learn how to rest in His presence

We have to learn to wait upon the Lord and not run off too soon. when we do, we will receive strength to do the impossible. Let's take a look at one of the last words Jesus spoke on this earth. Some folks emphasize that one of His last words was *go*. Yes, it is a very important word and it means to go into the world to spread the gospel. But one of the last words Jesus spoke was also *wait*.

> And I myself will send upon you what my Father has promised. But you must wait in the city until the power from above comes down upon you. (Luke 24:49 GNT)

What were His disciples waiting for? To be endued with power. Jesus had no intention to send His disciples out to fulfill the Great Commission without first giving them the power to accomplish it. And He doesn't want you to go or do something without it either.

We have to learn to wait upon the Lord for our Holy Spirit empowerment. If we will wait, trust, and hope in the Lord, then we shall mount up with wings of eagles, we shall run and not be weary, we shall walk and not faint!

In the New Living Translation, Isaiah 40:31 says, "Those who trust in the Lord will renew their strength." The New International Version says, "Those who hope in the Lord will renew their strength." Wait, trust, and hoping in the Lord will renew the strength you may have lost through the battles of life. Draw close to God today, and He will draw close to you—and BAM! He will empower you!

CONFESSION: Me and God got this today!

PRAYER

Father, I ask You to help me spend the necessary time required to renew my strength and help me focus on You. In Jesus' name, amen.

Day 53: The Battle at the Border

And whithersoever he entered, into villages, or cities, or country, they laid the sick in the streets, and besought him that they might touch if it were but the border of his garment: and as many as touched him were made whole. (Mark 6:56 KJV)

In the United States, immigration has always been a hot topic, especially, during election time or after an attack on our mainland. Every precaution is made or renewed to protect our borders from an invasion of illegal aliens or foreign armies.

The verse above tells the story (or stories) of multiple people who have been made whole by touching the "border" of Jesus garment. I'm not sure who gave them the idea of touching the border of His garment, but it seemed to work.

God honored the faith of those who pressed toward Him, those who crawled or elbowed their way to Him, or who crossed His path by accident and took advantage of the opportunity. They all battled to get to the border of his garment to receive their miracle. They fought the good fight of faith and won.

It's possible that they reached for the hem of His garment because of what it symbolized. In Jewish culture, people were instructed to put tassels on the hem of their garments, which represented the Word of God that they related to.

Give the following instructions to the people of Israel: Throughout the generations to come, you must make tassels for the hems of your clothing and attach them with a blue cord. When you see the tassels, you will remember and obey all the commands of the Lord instead of following your own desires and defiling yourselves, as you are prone to do. The tassels will help you remember that you must obey all my commands and be holy to your God. (Numbers 15:38-40 NLT)

So it's possible that the woman who had the issue of blood was inspired to press through the crowd in a last-ditch effort to be healed. According to the Law, she was considered unclean and would have been stoned if she were caught. But she was in faith and in agreement with the promises of the Word of God, and she was healed!

And, behold, a woman, which was diseased with an issue of blood twelve years, came behind him, and touched the hem of his garment: For she said within herself, if I may but touch his garment, I shall be whole. (Matthew 9:20-21 KJV)

Jesus responded to her by saying, "Your faith has healed you." You see, it was her faith that healed her; and healing can come to those who follow her example.

We don't have the physical body of Jesus walking on the earth today, but we do have the Word of God, both in Jesus and in the Bible. So are you fighting the good fight for healing? Then reach out and touch His Word, receive it as the Word of God, and receive your healing!

CONFESSION: I will fight the good fight of faith!

PRAYER

Jesus, You took the stripes on Your back and shed Your blood so I can receive healing power in my body. Lord, You created our bodies to heal themselves, but there are times when we need divine help, so we come boldly before Your throne and ask for it. Amen

Day 54: Do You Know What Temptation Is?

> And remember, when you are being tempted, do not say, "God is tempting me." God is never tempted to do wrong, and he never tempts anyone else. Temptation comes from our own desires, which entice us and drag us away. (James 1:13-14 NLT)

Temptation comes in all different sizes and shapes. But the meaning of the word *temptation* in the original Greek means: "A putting to proof."[12]

My first thought when I read that was the old saying, "the proof is in the pudding."

Temptation is ugly because it can be used to reveal where you are with God. It reveals your weaknesses as well as your strengths, just like taking a test at school. You don't learn anything by taking a test; it is a barometer of where you are in your learning process.

Planes go through various testing before they go on their maiden flight. One of them is that the wings are bent to a full 90 degrees under extreme pressure. Another interesting test is that the engines are tested by birds being launched into them by what they call "chicken guns." You can't make this stuff up!

The proof is in the putting. Every temptation you resist strengthens you as you prepare your future. If you fail in the temptation, it shows

---

12. "G3986 - peirasmos - Strong's Greek Lexicon (KJV)." Blue Letter Bible. Accessed 3 May, 2021. https://www.blueletterbible.org//lang/lexicon/lexicon.cfm?Strongs=G3986&t=KJV.

where you are at, and it should give you an urgency to strengthen that weak area in your life before the next temptation comes. Some temptations are easier to overcome than others. A key to overcoming temptation is recognizing that you are being tempted. I actually say, "Oh, I am being tempted!" I find that it really helps to vocalize it.

It would be great if we were tempted by some creature in a red suit, pointed tail, and a pitchfork. But it doesn't work that way. Besides, the devil isn't your worst enemy—you are!

Let's take a look where temptation comes from:

> Temptation comes from our own desires, which entice us
> and drag us away. (James 1:14 NLT)

Any time you are tempted, it will be in the area where you feel you have been deprived, where you are longing for something. That is the avenue where temptation parades on to get your soul's attention. Then the more you think about it, you will have conversations about it within yourself to justify it—to convince yourself that you deserve it. It has been withheld from you for too long, and now you feel you have a right to it and no one should stop you.

You will never be tempted by something you already have. For example, in America, we have a holiday called Thanksgiving Day. If you are not from American and are not familiar with this holiday, it is a day when family and friends gather for a special traditional family dinner. Ours is turkey dinner with all the trimmings. I personally make sure that there is canned cranberry sauce. The healthy kind has no business on my table. On Thanksgiving Day, most people will eat their full until they cannot put another bite into their mouths. If my wife would ask me immediately after dinner, "Danny, would you like a turkey sandwich?" I would put my hand up and say, "No way!" It would be very easy to resist in that moment because I just got done eating turkey. But if she asked me, "Honey, would like some apple pie?" Now she's got my attention. Guard yourself in these areas.

CONFESSION: I am a human being and I am prone to temptation!

PRAYER

I surrender my life to You, Holy Spirit, and I am so thankful for Your forgiveness. Holy Spirit, remind me when I am going to be tempted so I can battle it. In Jesus' name, amen.

Day 55: Do You Need Help Overcoming Temptation?

Y ou are not alone in this arena of temptation. Look what the Word says:

> The temptations in your life are no different from what others experience. (1 Corinthians 10:13 NLT)

You are not going through anything that your brothers and sisters in Christ have not experienced themselves. In other words, there's nothing new under sun that Satan or your own flesh can come up with to try to trip you up.

As long as you're living in a fleshly body, you will always be prone to temptation. That's because your fleshly body is very tuned-in to this world's environment. But the real battle, or should I say, the victory, takes place in your mind. Your thought life is the center of your emotions.

The good news is that the Word says we have the mind of Christ, according to 1 Corinthians 2:16. You must believe you have the mind of Christ, and secondly, you must learn to yield to the mind of Christ. "How can I do that," you may ask? It will happen when you make an inward decision in your spirit to live for God wholeheartedly. It's a paradigm shift and will not happen if you are halfhearted.

> And God is faithful. He will not allow the temptation to be more than you can stand. When you are tempted, he will show you a way out so that you can endure. (1 Corinthians 10:13)

The King James there says "escape." You may have to say, "Holy Spirit, show me the way of escape." If you wholeheartedly seek God,

He will open your spiritual eyes so you can see the escape route for your temptation.

I know, it's easier said than done. So I would like to suggest that you that build a support system for yourself. You do that by taking a good hard look at the people God has placed in your life. Then you ask the Holy Spirit who can help you in your walk with God. God may lead you to confide in a family member, a loyal friend, or even a spiritual leader you trust. If you are married, communicate with your spouse, or if you are not married then make an honest effort to find a support group. Lastly, go back to your basic training, and by that I mean your prayer closet. Matthew 26:41 says, "Watch and pray that ye enter not into temptation."

Many times when I have talked with people who were in a funk from falling into temptation, I would ask them, "Are you praying? Are you reading the Word, Are you getting good fellowship, or are you going to church?"

They would respond, "No, I'm not." But when they come back after of week of prayer, the Word, and church fellowship, they seem to be strong in the Lord and in the power of His might.

Satan will use your isolation against you and will scream lies at you. He will say, "You are so far gone, no one will respect you if you open up." That is the furthest thing from the truth! They may respect you more than ever before because of your honesty and openness. So remember this, Satan is a liar. He always has been and always will be, and he hates you with a passion. Ask the Holy Spirit to lead you to the right church, the right people, and the right person. Then trust yourself that you are hearing from God and follow through.

CONFESSION: I am not alone!

PRAYER

Father, in the name of Jesus I come against every lie satan has used against me. I put on the belt of truth and stand in your presence to cleanse my mind and shift into the mind of Christ. The mind of Christ says I am a child of God, I am washed by the blood of the Lamb, and my name is written in the Lamb's Book of Life. In Jesus' name, amen.

Day 56: Log Out!

Do not judge others, and you will not be judged. Do not condemn others, or it will all come back against you. Forgive others, and you will be forgiven. (Luke 6:37 NLT)

We need to stop judging others if we desire to have healthy relationships. If judgment, condemnation, and unforgiveness are in your life, your arteries are clogged and need to be cleaned out. It is stopping oxygen (the Holy Spirit) from flowing through your life.

If there is any place one should practice the "No Judging" zone, it's at home. Judging your teenager's and spouse's past behavior is really counterproductive. Oh, it's "great ammo" in the heat of the battle, but it's really futile in achieving lasting results.

Jean Marie and myself will be married forty-nine years this September. (to God be the glory, of course) Our marriage is far from perfect, but we are so much farther than we were in the past. There were times and seasons in the past when it didn't look like we were going to make it.

The past would always come up when we argued back then. Honestly, it was draining, tiring, and upsetting for both of us.

The good news is that we did something about it. We chose to get professional counseling. We were instructed to stop judging each other about our past behavior, and we took the advice. Oh, it wasn't easy, and we still argue, but it's nothing like it was twenty years ago. Now when we have a little cat-and-mouse match, we forget what we were arguing about a few minutes later. It has been so productive!

We actually enjoy each other's company more now than we ever did. We have truly become mates.

I would like to share some scripture that will cut to the heart. But if you are sincere about transforming into the image of Christ, this will cut will help you, not hurt you.

> And why worry about a speck in your friend's eye when you have a log in your own? How can you think of saying to your friend, "Let me help you get rid of that speck in your eye," when you can't see past the log in your own eye? Hypocrite! First, get rid of the log in your own eye; then you will see well enough to deal with the speck in your friend's eye. (Matthew 7:3-5 NLT)

Wow, right between the eyes! Trust me, when Jesus spoke this in His environment, surrounded by religious people, this cut bad. But remember Luke 6:37? Verse 38 continues on the same subject. Many preachers used this following scripture when taking up an offering. That's okay and true, but when Jesus first spoke about it, the context was about giving forgiveness to others who did you wrong. Let's read it:

> Give, and you will receive. Your gift will return to you in full—pressed down, shaken together to make room for more, running over, and poured into your lap. The amount you give will determine the amount you get back. (Luke 6:38 NLT)

My advice: Be forgiving and stop judging your kids, spouse, and others. Get the help you need and get ready to fight for the ones you love; peace will come.

CONFESSION: I will not judge anyone anymore!

PRAYER

Holy Spirit, in the name of Jesus, help me remove the log from my eye so I can help others remove the twig from theirs. Amen!

Day 57: Make Every Day Count

And the rest of the acts of Hezekiah, and all his might, and how he made a pool, and a conduit, and brought water into the city, are they not written in the book of the chronicles of the kings of Judah? (2 Kings 20:20 KJV)

This passage inspired me one morning in my devotions. I think it was Hezekiah's' ingenuity that grabbed my attention. The thought of bringing water into a city by building a conduit miles away would be a great accomplishment, even in these modern times. First, the idea had to come to him, then he had to find an engineering team to plan it, and he had to find the laborers to build it.

It must have been so exciting to see the results of this invention. I'm sure that they shouted when the water trickled down its path, and especially when someone took the first drink after filling their golden vessel. This invention was so amazing that even the Bible mentioned this accomplishment.

Why does this fascinate me so? Well, if you read what happens earlier in Hezekiah's' life, King Hezekiah was sicker than a dog, and he was dying. On top of that, all hope was removed when the Lord sent the Prophet Isaiah with a death sentence. The message went like this: "Set thine house in order; for thou shalt die and not live." Wow, what if a Man of God whom you trusted spoke that to you when you were sick?

The story goes on to say that when the king heard the prophet, he cried out to God, and then God listened to this good man's prayer, and God changed the death sentence by extending his life fifteen years. Not a bad deal for a dying man, huh?

Now back to the scriptures. The main reason I'm writing about this comes down to a question that came to my mind: was the pool and conduit built before or after the extension of his life? I'm not sure, but it caused me to think about my life. Like you, I want each day of my life to count. At this writing, I am on my 23,568th day on this earth, and how I wished that I hadn't wasted any of my days. The Word says: Teach us to number our days, that we may gain a heart of wisdom" (Psalm 90:12 NIV).

My heart is excited because I know that God is not through with my life. I know that I am the steward of the days I have left, and quite honestly, you and I cannot afford any more bad days. At this present time, God has granted us time to walk out our vision. For me, it is to "bring the River of Life to the people in Syracuse and beyond."

In closing, please read this next passage prayerfully with open your heart and mind and allow the Holy Spirit to lead you and guide you and teach you to make every day count!

> See then that ye walk circumspectly, not as fools, but as wise, Redeeming the time, because the days are evil. Wherefore be ye not unwise, but understanding what the will of the Lord is. (Ephesians 5:15-17)

CONFESSION: I cannot afford a bad day!

PRAYER

Father, we ask You in Jesus' name that You will stir us up in these last days and that we will live like it is our last day. Living with urgency and not in fear, but in faith, so we can accomplish the assignment that You have given us to do here on earth. In Jesus' name, amen.

Day 58: Being Moved by the Word of God

And it came to pass, when the king had heard the words of the book of the law, that he rent his clothes" (2 Kings 22:11 KJV)

King Josiah changed his generation from bad to good, from evil to righteous, and from Satan to God. He began to reign as king at a ripe old age of eight years old, and it appears he may have been between 18-26 years old when he had heard those words above.

Now most men's hormones are raging at that age, and with the false sensual religions that surrounded him, any young man would have easily been captivated by them. Yet when the Book of the Law was discovered after being hidden away for many years, he asked to have it read to him. While he listened, he was deeply moved by the Word of God. He was so intensely affected that he tore or "rent" his garments in two. That is much passion for a young man

Rending one's garments was an outward sign that someone was deeply moved and was determined to take action. Then he began to remove the idols out of the land and directed his kingdom to turn their head toward the Almighty God, and his nation was spared from God's wrath. It took much courage to do what he did at such a young age.

Allow me to you a few questions:

- What about yourself? When was the last time you were moved by the Word of God (the Bible)?

- Were you moved enough to "tear" your heart and cause a behavior change that ushered the grace of God to cover you and your loved ones?
- Are you waiting for others to go first?

Guess what? It's up to you. Yes, you! You will need to be brave and have great courage. Open your heart as you open your Bible, and ask the Holy Spirit to speak to you daily. Be ready to be moved by the Word of God.

There were many young people other than Josiah who were moved by the Word of God. To mention a few:

- Young Joseph was given prophetic dreams, which were fulfilled.
- David the shepherd boy who slew the giant and became king.
- Samuel the young boy who heard from God and became a judge and prophet.
- Don't forget the old people who were moved by the Word of God, like Moses, who was eighty years old when he was called to lead a nation.
- Zacharias and Elizabeth gave birth at an old age in obedience to the Word of God
- Don't forget Abraham and Sarah, who birthed Isaac at a ripe old age of one hundred and ninety.

Keep your heart right before God and keep the last thing John wrote: "Little children, keep yourselves from idols" (1 John 5:21 KJV).

CONFESSION: I will serve King Jesus!

PRAYER

I ask You, Lord, to help me crave the Word of God as a newborn baby does milk. Lord, more importantly, give me the desire to please You in every way that I can. I know You died for me and forgave me of all of my sins. I ask You to give me the grace that is needed to live a life of obedience and to walk in the power of Your Spirit. Allow me to be courageous like the young King Josiah was so I can be a leader of my generation. In Jesus' name, amen.

Day 59: Can I Walk on Water?

M atthew pens down a story about Jesus walking on water:

> And Peter answered him and said, Lord, if it is thou, bid
> me come unto thee on the water. And he said, Come. And
> when Peter was come down out of the ship, he walked on
> the water, to go to Jesus. (Matthew 14:28-29 KJV)

It is very interesting that Peter did the same thing Jesus did after he heard Jesus say, "come." One four-letter word: Come.

Most of us know the rest of the story about how when Peter saw the boisterous waves and felt the wind, he was afraid and began to sink. Did Peter fail? Yes and no. Remember, the other eleven disciples remained in the boat as Peter stepped out in faith. He began well, but in this story, he didn't end well. There is such thing as the starting anointing, but unfortunately, not everyone will have the finishing anointing. Hopefully, this story will help you so the situation that you are facing today can end well.

As I read this, I'm thinking to myself, What would "walking on water" do for me?" Well, I could get paid minimum wage as a lifeguard at a beach. Or I could get a gig at Las Vegas, or I could even walk across the Atlantic to Europe. But then I thought, "That's almost like walking from Syracuse NY to the end tip of the state of Florida. That is a long way; I think I would rather fly.

Let's do this: if we substituted the words *walking on water*, and replace them with words like *building your business*, *getting your degree*, *working on your marriage*, and *getting our children through the teenage years and into college*, it would seem to be of greater value, doesn't it?

171

Questions:

- What word or promise has the Lord spoken to you?
- Did Jesus, through the Holy Spirit, say to you what He had said to Peter? "Come?' Or even "GO?"
- Do you have a sinking feeling like your going down and you and your God-dream has sunk?

And immediately Jesus stretched forth his hand, and caught him, and said unto him, O thou of little faith, wherefore didst thou doubt? (Matthew 14:31 KJV)

I suggest that you go back to that Word He has spoken to you to do. As Kenneth Copeland says: "One Word From God can save your life." So be strong and of good courage and fulfill the Word of the Lord in your life.

CONFESSION: I will do what You say, Lord!

PRAYER

Father, I come to You in the name of Jesus Christ, Your Son, the One who shed His blood to establish your covenant with us—a better covenant. You assured us that You are not a man that You can lie. You have integrity, Father, and so does the Word You have spoken to me. If I am confused, Lord, help me find godly leaders I can get good counsel from, for I know Your Word says that there is safety in the multitude of them. Lord, if I know that I know that I heard from You, I ask that I can be strong in the grace of God, so after doing all that I can do, I will be able to stand on Your Word. In Jesus' name, amen.

Day 60: The Magnetic Pull of God's Presence

Send out your light and your truth; let them guide me.
(Psalms 43:3 NLT)

I have always been astonished at how magnets work. Seeing them in operation as a young child was fascinating. I would go around the house with a magnet and see what I could find to stick it on, and when I did, I would put it on, take it off and put it back on again, and repeat the process. With my possessive personality, you can only imagine how long I did that.

Sometimes I would put it close to a metal object and not touch it to feel the magnetic pull between the magnet and the object. But the pull was always stronger than my finesse in keeping them separate, and then—click; they were joined together again.

Take a look at this scripture, and I dare you not to see the science behind the pull of the magnet and our loving God drawing close to us:

Draw nigh to God, and he will draw nigh to you.
(James 4:8 KJV)

This again is another classic example of the transfer of GodStrength that is available to anyone who will draw close to God.

The transfer of His strength is evident if we will look at the scripture that comes before that one:

> Submit yourselves therefore to God. Resist the devil, and
> he will flee from you. (James 4:7 KJV)

I see this as God telling us that we have no power ourselves to resist the power of satan. The Holy Spirit admonishes us to submit or draw close to God Almighty so we will have His strength to resist the devil. Look at this; the devil recognizes the power of God in us, and he will flee from us. To *flee* means to run away. He will run away from us because of the anointing on our lives.

How can I do this in a practical way? I encourage you to read the Word of God, spend time in prayer with Jesus, and obey the Holy Spirit in the little things so you can obey when the big things come up. Find a house of God that preaches the Word, and get some corporate fellowship. Simply spend time with God, and He will draw close to you. It is as much a spiritual law as the law of gravity is a natural law; both have a pull. One upward, the other downward.

Warning: (I'm staying with the analogy of the magnets) Have you ever noticed how two magnets repel from each other when you place them together a certain way?

Yes, I have a scripture for that too:

> Wherefore he saith, God resisteth the proud.
> (James 4:6 KJV)

Resisteth in the Greek means "to arrange, organize, or plan oneself against." Wow! When we are filled with pride, God arranges plans against us so we will come to our knees.

How is your ego? Is it inflated? Has God reminded you recently about a situation when you acted like a proud peacock prancing around and taking credit for something?

SOAR IN HIS STRENGTH

Are you thinking, "Well, God, if I am proud, please humble me?" That's something you don't want God to do! But God has put that responsibility into your hands.

> Humble yourselves in the sight of the Lord, and he shall lift you up. (James 4:10 KJV)

CONFESSION: Lord, I am coming to You, so You will come to me!

PRAYER

Lord, I humble myself to You. I am nothing without You; I can do nothing without You. I can only do what You have called me to do. I thank You for Your grace in my life as I humble myself to You. In Jesus' name, amen.

About the Author

D anny Thornton married his high-school sweetheart, Jean Marie, and forty-eight years later, they are still enjoying married life. They have two grown daughters and six beautiful grandchildren who are even now teaching, preaching, serving, and worshipping in the vibrant church they founded in 1990: River Church in Syracuse, New York.

Danny is proud of his two gospel sons: Dan Allen, who pastors River Church in Syracuse, New York, and Justin Metcalf, who pastors Solid Rock Church in Albany, New York. Danny passed the baton to his gospel son in Syracuse, keeping apostolic oversight of the church

Danny launched GodStrength.Coach™ to empower pastors, leaders, and congregations in living life through God's strength and not their own.

The Thornton's deepest passions are to see pastors and ministry leaders and their families be healed, whole, and positioned into the places God by the transfer of God's Strength.

Danny can be contacted at godstrength.coach@yahoo.com.

About GodStrength.Coach

We are of the belief that God promises his children strength. God-Strength.Coach (GS) is a designed to usher the transfer of God's strength to those who desire it.

This is done in a number of practical ways:

- GodStrength for Today short video inspirations and Thought for Today power quotes on multimedia.

- Literature like The 9 Spiritual Fronts and Soar in His Strength, Volume 1, which is made up of sixty inspirational devotions designed to strengthen your walk with God.

- Men's Breakfast of Champions, held once a month. We ask our fellow champions from the corporate world or champions from the Christian community to share their testimony with the hope of bringing men and women to Christ.

- If you prefer ministry in a more personal matter, GS offers life coaching sessions that empowers individuals or groups to help guide them in fulfilling their assignment and launching them into their destiny.

- GodStrength Conferences: geared toward leaders, believers, and worshippers.

- For qualified individuals who are active in ministry, we license and ordained those who desire to network with GS.

Follow GS on Facebook, Twitter (@GodStrength2), Instagram (thunder_thornton_), or by mail:

GodStrength.Coach
P.O. Box 2573
Liverpool NY 13090

CPSIA information can be obtained
at www.ICGtesting.com
Printed in the USA
JSHW041557230521
15077JS00003B/4